God rides
a Yamaha

Kathy Shaidle

God rides a Yamaha

Musings on pain, poetry and pop culture

Northstone

Northstone Publishing acknowledges the financial support of the Government of Canada through the Book Publishing Industry Development Program for its publishing activities.

Northstone Publishing is an imprint of Wood Lake Books Inc., an employee-owned company, and is committed to caring for the environment and all creation. Northstone recycles, reuses, and composts, and encourages readers to do the same. Resources are printed on recycled paper and more environmentally friendly groundwood papers (newsprint), whenever possible. The trees used are replaced through donations to the Scoutrees for Canada program. Ten percent of all profit is donated to charitable organizations.

Printing 10 9 8 7 6 5 4 3 2 1
Printed in Canada by
Transcontinental Printing

Editors: Michael Schwartzentruber,
Dianne Greenslade
Cover and interior design: Margaret Kyle
Consulting art director: Robert MacDonald

Grateful acknowledgment is made to the following for permission to reprint copyrighted material: Quotations from "Bone Poems" in *Night Field* by Don McKay. Used by permission, McClelland & Stewart, Inc. *The Canadian Publishers*. Quotations from *New Seeds of Contemplation* by Thomas Merton. Used by permission of New Directions Publishing Corp. Copyright © 1961 The Abbey of Gethsemani, Inc.

Canadian Cataloguing in Publication Data
Shaidle, Kathy, 1964–
God rides a Yamaha

ISBN 1-896836-24-0
1. Shaidle, Kathy, 1964– 2. Systemic lupus
erythematosus –
Patients – Biography. I. Title.
RC924.5.L85S52 1998   362.1'9677   C98-910632-2

Published by Northstone Publishing,
an imprint of Wood Lake Books Publishing Inc.
Kelowna, British Columbia, Canada

Contents

2

God and the single girl

Beyond the fringe

My so-called life

"Quitting your day job" is every artist's dream. Mine came true in 1991, when some government arts grants let me write full-time.

Six weeks later, I contracted systemic lupus erythematosus, an incurable, life-threatening disease.

I'd always smugly agreed with Stephen King that "a little irony is good for the blood." Someone else's blood, that is. An artsy armchair outlaw, I'd cultivated a connoisseur's nose for Tragedy, Absurdity, And The Strange Beauty Of Ugliness And Pain.

So it was poetic justice that the attendant ironies of my condition were as burdensome as my illness itself.

During a recession, I'd quit a perfectly good "real" job to write poetry. Now, as everyone knows, "writing" isn't really "work" – and "writing poetry" less so. When criticized for "just wanting to sit around all day," I'd passionately protested. Not because this was false, mind you, but because it was true.

I'd worked since my 16th birthday, through college and beyond, mostly for men half as smart as me who made twice as much money. I felt entitled, at age 26, to savor the irresponsible extended adolescence I'd missed.

So (my protests to the contrary) I planned to "write/do nothing" a bit, and "goof off/do nothing" a lot.

Six months after my diagnosis, I could do neither (see "poetic justice" above). Bedridden by arthritis, I used all the free time I'd planned to spend "doing nothing" doing nothing but morbidly pondering my Incredible Shrinking Life.

I soon realized that all my book learning and adolescent anarchism had undone my "work til you die" socialization not a whit. What did it profiteth me that I'd virtually memorized Thomas Merton's ode to doing nothing, *A Signed Confession of Crimes Against The State*? Couldn't recall a bloody word when my long-suffering mother asked shyly, "Do you think you'll ever work again, dear?"

And I'd screech through gritted teeth: " I AM working, MU-THER!"

Meaning "writing." Which I wasn't even. Which isn't, even. "Working", that is.

I was a poet. On disability. I basically did nothing. Twice.

I eventually grew tired of, tired from, doing nothing. So I took up "doing nothing" in earnest. Or instead, if you like.

I took up contemplative prayer. If only in terms of cosmic economics, I was still, I believe, contributing some mysterious something to the world.

My world, meanwhile, had shrunk to four walls, within which brewed an ever-growing mess.

Because housework was painfully impossible. On my rare good days, my biggest accomplishment was doing some laundry.

I'd been reduced to being...just a housewife. And I wasn't even married! My family's women have worked outside the home for generations; neither *Cosmo*, *Donahue*, or *Police Woman* had prepared me (the "smart one in the family," its first liberated college girl) for this reluctant '50s flashback. There's no Nobel Prize for Housework, I'd mutter. Ambushed by yet another irony.

Then I developed myositis on top of my lupus. Prednisone was prescribed and I moved without pain for the first time that year.

When movie burn victims remove their facial bandages, they always shout, "Give me a mirror!" Post-prednisone, my first words were, "Give me a pen!" I started scribbling, nonsense mostly. My handwriting stared up at me, a long-lost child, shaky, a little sheepish, but alive.

I could write again. So I did.

Catholic New Times hired me to write about chronic illness. As their former production manager, I knew the paper well, and tried to give my columns a "social justice" spin.

But my illness had made me very small (I weighed 85 lbs.) and my world had shrunk in sympathy, leaving no room for politics or propaganda. It was ridiculous to blame my lupus on the Bush Administration, to apply Marxist analysis to the task of opening juice bottles when my hands were swollen stumps.

So I stopped trying. I wrote about my latest hairdo, or watching *Oprah*! I was surprised and gratified by the volume of fan mail I received.

But as Jesus would say, you just can't win. Seems I'd lacked the good taste and foresight to be born in Central America, so (to a few) my suffering wasn't "political" and my columns, therefore, "too personal."

So...I was "working" again. Meaning "writing," albeit from the fringes of a fringe-to-begin-with paper. But, to a minority, my "personal" stuff wasn't "real writing"; some poets who'd known me only as one of their number agreed; and society didn't consider any of my writing (poetry or prose) "real work" at all.

"My mother says to get a job," sing neo-punks Green Day, "but she don't like the one she's got." I feel guilty when I think of those my age who've made careers out of unemployment. Gee! I got to be a fashionable "slacker" without even lifting a finger.

Because I couldn't lift a finger.

I could in remission though, and applied for "real" jobs. So did a hundred others – whose résumés presumably didn't crash at 1991 like mine.

I'm not in remission now. Three drugs are used to treat lupus. As of today, I'm on all of them. The latest may fix my fatigue. Too soon to tell. Chloroquine takes six weeks to start "working." Pretty lazy for "fatigue pills," huh? But seriously folks, the good news is that, according to the Canadian Prescription Guide, it will take chloroquine a little longer than six weeks to make me go totally blind!!

(Just what the world needs. Another blind poet. Homer. Milton. Me.)

These drugs can only (maybe) restore me to 80 percent normal. If that number sounds pretty good to you, amputate 20 percent of yourself and call me in the morning. From your "real" job. (If they let you keep it.) The kind of job I said I never wanted, and now may never have again.

My invisible disease is my invisible job: full-time, on-call, mine 'til I die. One which requires no education or experience and which pays accordingly.

On the news today, the Japanese goverment announced their earthquake compensation plan: $50,000 for "dead breadwinners." Half that for "anyone else." Self-centered in the extreme, I wonder what small change my death might bring.

One chapter in Laura Chester's memoir *Lupus Novice* is titled "Disaster, Called A Vacation."

I misread that at first as Vocation.

We were both right all along.

✠ ✠ ✠

Shortly after I wrote those words in 1995 (for a special issue of *Compass* on "Work"), I was offered a full-time job – by, of all people, another *Catholic New Times* alumnus. (Catholic publishing's a lot like the "Hotel California"; you can check out any time you like, but you can never leave.)

My doctors were confident that I was well enough to re-enter the workforce, and my "Disability" workers assured me I'd be back on their rolls immediately if my doctors turned out to be wrong. And I was stronger than ever, felt better than I had before I'd gotten sick.

Still, the first six months were overwhelming, but not physically (unless you count the ingrown toenail I developed from wearing dress shoes for the first time in years).

My emotional stability was another matter. I'd never been a poster child for mental health, but emerging from years of profound solitude shocked my system. Twelve-hour days, nicotine withdrawal, and a precipitous learning curve (years of softwear upgrades, and a week to catch up!) didn't help.

I was overwhelmed. Something had to give, and that something turned out to be my *CNT* column. Even if I hadn't run out of time and energy to write, I had, after four years, run out of anything else to say.

And that's about how I feel now, too. Writing a conclusion to an introduction is just as tricky as it sounds. I can't sign off without a few words of thanks:

to all at *CNT*, for your faith, encouragement and yes, even and especially for your criticism. You made me a better writer in spite of myself

to my "constant readers," whose kind calls and letters always came just when I was about to give up

and to all the friends I can't believe I have, and certainly don't deserve. As outward signs of God's grace, you are proof that friendship is the eighth sacrament.

1

Confessions
of a
bearded
lady

Man Alive talks to chronic
pain sufferers and the
author talks to a friend

I've fallen
and I can't get up

Gazing up into the darkness
 I saw myself as a creature driven and
derided by vanity; and my eyes burned with
anguish and anger.

JAMES JOYCE, *ARABY*

I sit in the usual pub at the usual time, waiting for my usual
friend. Thursday night. *Simpsons* night. At 8 p.m., the propri-
etors of the Beverly Tavern switch both TVs from boxing to
that ultra-hip cartoon show. My friend and I have taken to
meeting here on Queen Street West to giggle at Homer and
Marge and Bart.

It's about the only ritual I can take right now.

I'm early, still alone. What to do? I could be a good little writer and go over the notes to the *Man Alive* show I said I'd review for *Catholic New Times*.

Nope...

Instead, I open the book I just bought. *Lupus Novice* by Laura Chester.

Man Alive's "It Only Hurts" episode opens in a Toronto gym. While two boxers pummel each other in the background, host Peter Downie explains that "11 percent of Canadians suffer from chronic pain." And, "In our society, being strong isn't what we can dish out, it's what we can take."

Last summer, I woke up the Morning After a particularly gruesome Night Before, looked in the mirror, and didn't recognize myself. If that was a sunburn, then why was it confined to my nose and cheeks, in the shape of one of those Hallowe'en-masks-on-a-stick you'd see in *Amadeus*?

When the neon-pink "stain" didn't go away, I stomped off to the local clinic. I was probably just allergic to something – not beer, I hoped – or just going to too many parties. There was nothing wrong with me. Sure, I'd once been an early riser and now could barely crawl out of bed. And I found it hard to swallow, but then again I had been smoking a lot.

But this was too much – this was my face. I had dates to go on, people to meet. I had just turned 27, had just started writing full-time and I had nothing but time and money and sunshine on my hands.

Nothing could be wrong with me.

I entered the doctor's office and declared in my most imperious, Bette Davis voice: "Do something about my face, will you? I can't possibly be seen like this."

And the doctor replied, "What do you know about lupus?"

The *Man Alive* episode focuses on two chronic pain sufferers.

Mike is a former construction worker who threw his back out on the job. Accustomed to defining himself by his very physical, even "macho" work, Mike feels demoralized by his new job of house-husband.

Joanne was also felled by a back injury. A former nurse, Joanne is haunted by memories of her old job; she and other nurses taunted patients in pain, especially those who'd buzz for more medication.

"We'd flick off the switch (at the nurses' station) and say, 'Let them wait a few minutes.'"

Today, Joanne walks with a cane.

I flip through *Lupus Novice* as I wait for my friend, and develop an instant dislike for Ms. Chester, an Earth Mother New Ager who probably grows her own tofu. Actually, I don't think I'd have liked her or her book regardless: I spend half my time digging up all the information I can about lupus, and the other half feeling cranky about what I've read.

Ms. Chester has apparently tried every holistic, icky-sounding cure this side of Tibet. When I get to the chapter on her daily coffee enemas, I decide it's time for another beer.

When the doctor asked me that question about lupus last summer, I froze. My aunt used to volunteer for the Lupus Association. I flashed back to my adolescence, when my cousin tried to explain what the organization did. Being the know-it-all teenager I was (as opposed to the know-it-all adult I am now) I snorted, "There's no such thing as 'lupus,' Andrea. I mean, I've never heard of it!" Now I was being punished for that asinine comment.

And I'm a nominally Catholic writer, and lupus killed Flannery O'Connor, who died the year I was born. For years I'd assured myself, being a good little surrealist, that there is no such thing as coincidence. As the doctor droned on about "arthritis" and "photosensitivity" and "the onset of kidney failure," I could only wish I'd latched on to something nice and harmless like minimalism instead.

"We tend to believe in the nobility of suffering," Downie says. "That it's somehow 'weak' to take drugs. We see pain as a contest, and when we can't take it anymore, we feel like quitters."

Joanne went to the same emergency ward so many times, seeking relief from her aching back, that the staff decided she was a Demerol junkie and sent her to the psychiatric ward.

The show's litany continues: operations that do more harm than good, strained or disintegrated marriages, suicide attempts.

Downie says, "There is no objective way to measure another person's pain."

Mark bounces into the pub and gives me a little paper rose. I use it for a bookmark and shove *Lupus Novice* into my purse.

"Whatcha reading?" he asks.

I quickly ask about his day, trying to smile, trying so hard to listen. Sure, *The Simpsons* will cheer me up, and Mark is always great company. But I can already feel my knees stiffening. It's only 7:30 and I'll be ready to collapse in two hours; this after sleeping all day just to be "up" for tonight. And I keep thinking about my follow-up appointment at Wellesley Hospital two weeks from now, when I'll be answering "yes" to the old "no" questions: Does your pain wake you in the night? Have your feet turned blue?

What polish, I wonder, doesn't clash with purple toes?

"How are you feeling?" Mark asks.

I just shrug. Or try to – my shoulder bites back.

"Christ, I can't even shrug anymore," I reply. "And that was one of my major gestures."

My friends understand the I'm-a-tough-broad-who-speaks-in-italics routine I use to discuss my illness. But I wonder how much longer they'll put up with all this.

Man Alive again.

Diane leads a support group for "pain people." I have to laugh. In ten years there'll be an Oprah show about "Adult Children of Pain People." I hate cute euphemisms. I hate this show. I hate myself.

I watch *Man Alive* at home, alone, notebook in hand, but unopened, smoking too many cigarettes. If anyone thinks I'm quitting now, they're nuts. I tune in and out of the program, lost in my own thoughts. Stuck in my own head. Head. One lupus symptom I don't have yet is hair loss. Thank God. But I think about wigs anyway. A nice Park Avenue bouffant. My aesthetic ideal – a perfect little helmet.

Diane writes letters to her pain. Diane tried to kill herself, but then remembered her child. Diane has a son. She no longer has a husband.

The Simpsons makes me laugh, as usual, heartily and right out loud. Real Norman Cousins stuff, I tell myself. *Anatomy of an Illness*, "laugh yourself well" and all that.

Unfortunately, the good feeling is short-lived. My friend asks again how I feel. And his concern makes me crumble, besides the fact that *Losing My Religion* comes blaring through the speakers – the only song in the world about everything that ever has and ever will happen.

"Of all the gin joints..." I mutter.

And then I'm crying, right in the middle of the stupid Beverly Tavern. I can't be seen like this.

Mark moves beside me and holds my hand.

"It's not fair," I whisper. "This body of mine hasn't exactly brought me lots of luck. I'm not Miss America here. But just when I was starting to like my body, when I finally stopped being an ugly duckling...Bang! It turned on me again.

"I'm too young to be an old lady! Okay, so Elizabeth Barrett Browning started this way, but still...

"Geez, can't they play another song? Maybe *Don't Get Around Much Anymore...*?"

Joanne says, "If life gives you lemons, make lemonade."

Great. Now we've entered the Bumper Sticker School Of Philosophy.

I can't help but think about the bad TV my life would make. I'm not a likeable, disease-movie-of-the-week heroine, pretty in a plain sort of way, running marathons or whatever in spite of my incurable illness. I'm not even as serene or just plain likeable as Mike or Joanne or Diane on *Man Alive*.

I smoke and drink and bleach my hair and wear too much

make-up. I sometimes wish I could be one of those acceptable heroines I grew up watching. But mostly, right now, I'm just pissed off. Which is not a "nice" way to feel when you're basically a Professional Catholic.

Speaking of which: pray? Don't ask. I'm just too angry right now, and besides, it hurts my knees. (But seriously, folks...) I know I'm a vain, proud woman and prayer involves submission and humility.

Which would do me a lot of good.

Unfortunately, just getting out of bed is humiliating enough.

It's hard to run from The Hound of Heaven when you're wearing high-heeled boots, but I have to. I just have to. For a little while longer.

When God really wants me, finding me won't be a problem. God's done it before.

I'm sorry if this isn't very inspirational. I can barely hold a pen to write.

On *Man Alive*, Dr. Ron Melzac of McGill has the last word:

We all fight very hard for our dignity. None of us likes to be in the position where we are vulnerable, and part of that dignity is lost when we cry out in pain.

What astonishes me always is the inherent courage

of these people, and they are a reflection of all mankind. They reflect the courage we somehow are able to muster up in these situations.

Mark finally gets a word in. "So you've got sore knees sometimes. So what? I'm your friend. I want to take care of you. I can't stand the idea of you going home alone like this. Come to my place and crash on the couch. Please."

"No way. You have to work at six in the morning, and I've got an appointment tomorrow. Let's just get the hell outta here."

One nice thing about lupus is the photosensitivity, which means I get to wear sunglasses whenever I want. Totally cool. I consider shoving mine on for the long walk to the exit, to hide my red eyes and smeared mascara from the hip trendies in the Bev. Oh, forget it. Let 'em eat life.

With some difficulty, I zip up the black biker jacket I bought the day after my official diagnosis. If I was gonna be sick, I would do it with style. I've left it on all night, not to be fashionable, but because it hurts my arms too much to take it off.

Right – armor intact, and I'm ready to roll. Sure, it's an armor of hairspray and leather, and plastic, but the only alternative is all-too-vulnerable flesh, and I know the load of good *that* does.

Mark leaps up. His energy never ceases to amaze me. I, on the other hand, ease myself out of my chair, relieved that the loud music is covering up the sound of my cracking bones. Everyone in the place probably thinks I'm drunk.

We both walk out onto Queen Street and my streetcar rattles into view.

"Hey, I forgot! You can't run," says Mark. With that, he picks me up and carries me across the road to the streetcar. "Always the gentleman," he smiles at me (and to himself, well aware of the absurdity of a "gentleman" with a Mohawk) as we hug goodbye hurriedly.

On the streetcar, I stare out the window, watching people walk, even run, with such ease. And suddenly I just start laughing. So glad to have a good friend, to be going home to bed. "Sleep," wrote Flannery O'Connor, "is the mother of God."

But there's something else inside the laugh, a bitter catch I've heard before. This isn't the laugh of a clean-cut saint who can take anything the world, or God, can dish out.

It's rather the laugh of, say, a woman who finds herself standing in the middle of a dark, dingy room long after the party's over. Wondering where her shoes are.

Wondering how she got there.

"You know I'm an agnostic," Mark said once. "But I don't understand. I thought people like you, when they had a problem, took comfort in their religion."

"So did I," I replied.

Confessions of a bearded lady

My lupus drugs, particularly the steroid prednisone, have granted me two blessedly pain-free months.

Unfortunately, drugs mean side effects. "Special effects" more like! Prednisone-induced Jekyll and Hyde transformations are more distressing to some lupus patients than their former fatigue and arthritis. At least pain is "invisible."

Consider this young woman in my Lupus Support Group, who's getting married this winter: "My doctor wants me on steroids, but I've heard I'll gain weight. What about my expensive fitted gown when December comes? And the photos?

I won't look like myself, and those pictures can't be taken again!"

I try to combine humor and common sense to cope with side effects. My low-fat, low-salt diet keeps bloating away. I instructed friends to call me The Chipmunk of Notre Dame when the prednisone-promised "moon face" and fatty back hump appeared; but so far, I'm no Quasimodo, and my facial swelling actually makes skinny me look healthier.

Another side effect posed a bigger challenge.

I'd spent weeks explaining that prednisone isn't a steroid of the anabolic, Ben Johnson variety and fielding lots of Terminator jokes. (Although, my MedicAlert necklace's resemblance to an Olympic silver medal is enhanced by the words "On Steroids" engraved on the back.)

Okay, so no hormones, right?

And what (as I'd been warned) happened?

I grew a beard.

My friends insist they can't see it. (That's why they're my friends.) But the hair's there. What to do?

That modern Zen master, St. Thérèse of Lisieux, offered a solution. Her meditation was disturbed by another sister grinding her teeth. Thérèse considered angrily confronting the offender, then tried to simply ignore the noise, but only succeeded in breaking out in a sweat under the effort. Finally: "I concentrated on listening to it as though it were a magnificent concert."

I too was tempted to throw daily temper tantrums, or to just ignore the hair (and my feelings).

Finally, working up "the courage to change the things I can," I bought bleach, as embarrassing a purchase for me as hemorrhoid cream for someone else. Heck, I've dyed my "hair" hair for years – why not just do my whole head? And just think: in this recession, I'm keeping dozens of Jolen Creme Bleach workers gainfully employed.

I also remembered my heroines. Photographers say that Marilyn Monroe's excessive blonde facial down reflected light and made her more photogenic. And painter Frida Kahlo, considered one of Mexico's most beautiful women, had one long eyebrow and a thick black moustache. Her self-portraits show off these "flaws," and photographs show a laughing, beautifully dressed woman, clearly pleased with herself and life.

Besides, I'm just too busy to waste much time morbidly pondering my sudden resemblance to a baby chicken.

So if you'll excuse me, the full moon calls. That howling sound you hear isn't a werewolf. It's only me.

Walk softly and carry a big prayer

I don't need a cane (yet) but I want one anyway. Mostly so I can paint it pink, stick a really loud bicycle bell on top, and use it to hit people.

Seriously...Like many people with arthritis, young and old, I've developed an acute fear of falling that's aggravated by winter's slippery streets. I'm actually forced to patronize different stores depending on the season, because certain merchants leave their sidewalks as unsalted as bake-sale popcorn (see "hit people," above). So just imagine having something sturdy to lean on when negotiating those unshoveled sidewalks and steps.

Actually, a steady, comforting cane would serve more as a psychological aid. Worse than the ice itself is that inner voice screaming, "Hey, check out that ice! Sure is lots of ice up ahead! Rev up that Zamboni, we're talkin' Ice City, USA!

"Whatever you do, don't fall!"

Veritable psychic banana peels.

I really need a "brain cane," sturdy words to walk with, to poke those banana peels out of my path.

✣ ✣ ✣

Saint Paul exhorts us to pray constantly.

He also wants me to wear a hat.

And I do not wear hats.

When the poor man says something I don't like, I'm quick to dismiss him, but hey, even a stopped clock is right twice a day.

Metropolitan Anthony Bloom (who's right all day long) calls the Orthodox Jesus Prayer, "more or less continuous, a vocal prayer that serves as a background, a walking-stick, throughout the day..."

"Walking-stick" is right. As explained in *The Way of a Pilgrim*, the Jesus Prayer ("Lord Jesus Christ, Son of God, have mercy on me, a sinner") keeps time with the pilgrim's footsteps and heartbeat.

Footsteps: the prayer's tap-tap-tap was just the "brain cane" I was looking for.

And heartbeat: I was reminded of Norman Cousin's description of laughter as "intestinal jogging." This "prayer of the heart" as it's sometimes called, could be my "soul aerobics" while I exercised my legs.

How hard could it be? After all, hadn't I, like millions of others, managed to hum, effortlessly and involuntarily throughout the day, the very last song I'd heard on drive-time radio just before leaving for work? (And hadn't I, like millions of others, wondered why That Song was, invariably, Barry Manilow's *Copacabana*?)

I found the original Jesus Prayer a bit unwieldy, so I switched to the sufficiently cane-like 23rd Psalm (all that "rod and staff" stuff) but discarded that prayer as too, well, funereal. Like *Auld Lang Syne*, "The Lord is my Shepherd" always makes me think of the Titanic – hardly reassuring when crashing into ice is what you're trying to avoid.

After reading everything from *The Cloud of Unknowing* to *The Power of Positive Thinking*, I'd tried so many suggested "Christian mantras" that my soul was more addled than calmed, more Baskin-Robbins than basilica.

This week I've settled on "I do all things through Christ which strengtheneth me" (Philippians 4:13).

That's right: Mr. All-Things-To-All-Men and I are back

on speaking terms. Besides (to paraphrase the kids on *American Bandstand*) it's got a good beat and you can walk to it.

So now I've got my Jesus Prayer.

But I still don't have a real cane.

And no matter how cold and snowy it gets outside, Paul or no Paul, I'm still not wearing a hat.

Wake up and smell the Advent coffee

I've had my liturgical colors done and an Advent I ain't.

Guess I'm an armchair Carmelite, more attracted to Lent's austerity, discipline and high drama as only a lazy coward could be. ("I've been kneeling for five whole minutes! Look out St. Teresa!")

Or blame my – ahem – aesthetic sensibility, that irrepressible urge to draw a mustache on the Mona Lisa; Lent's a penitential beauty mark on spring's peaches and cream complexion.

Advent's the opposite: a forced smile at winter's lousy joke.

Maybe I'm so submerged in society's "death culture" that I can't get into the nativity. Agatha Christie didn't get rich writing "birth mysteries." And, unlike violent TV shows such as *America's Most Wanted*, a "reality program" called, say, *Lamaze Class USA!* would die in the ratings. Pun intended.

But oh, how a mother with a baby changes everything, or should. Bus seats offered, voices lowered. Eyes light up, we snap awake. Or do we?

Like the other day, browsing in a Catholic bookstore's "Daily Meditations: Advent" section – this year, finally getting myself all holied up for Christmas.

What a great day. My "To Do" list was studded with checkmarks. Back home, my VCR was taping a talk show: "Apparitions of the Virgin Mary." Good for a laugh, to watch later that evening over another great meal courtesy of Mom. (She'd come from Hamilton last week, laden with food, despite the cast on her arm. I really have to remember to mail her that thank-you card.)

Meanwhile, I flipped through the Advent books. I'd add this religious discipline to the growing list of Things I Do To Make Myself An Even More Wonderful Human Being.

Maybe I'd even write a column about it, so everyone could read about my utter fabulosity.

If only that person outside the store would cut out that infernal, clanging racket. I needed to concentrate.

I heard a help-requesting "Hel-lo-o!?" in the distance. Pretended I hadn't.

Bang!

I jumped at the glassy crash behind me, but didn't, couldn't turn around. The bookstore's front door, I guessed. Practically kicked open.

Someone doesn't know their own strength.

"Damn you people!" a woman shouted from the doorway behind me. I froze even harder in place. As she shouted I stared stupidly at the festive book covers within my field of vision.

"Didn't you see me tryin' to get this stroller down those stairs? I only got one good arm here! Call yourselves Christians too busy readin' books about Jesus to help a one-armed woman with a baby!"

A child cries. Hurried shuffling, whispered apologies. The door squeaks open, then clicks closed, to the silence I'd thought I'd wanted.

Having an illness which (at least now) doesn't allow me to work gives me the time and inclination to re-evaluate my life and make changes. Too bad I'm so busy "working on myself" that I ignore others.

Turning down the phone to meditate, keeping it down in case somebody calls with a "problem." What good is my physiotherapy if I don't use my healthy hands to help someone? Why work and pray for remission only to be remiss in healing others?

Whosoever seeks to save his life...

Keep awake therefore...

But I'm a sleepy shepherd, responding to the herald angels' "Hark!" with a yawning, "Maybe later."

So I hit the snooze button on the Advent alarm clock, pull up the covers when the baby cries. There's also Advent's theme of patience – we wait in joyful hope – me? My picture of Hell is an eternal doctor's waiting room. With only one *Newsweek*.

I want everything my own way, and want my own "perfection" now. Lupus means symptoms and side effects that vary daily, and I hate surprises. I can't flow with these liturgical seasons either, their changing weather. I want stasis, a mild, predictable Vancouver of the soul.

That Marian visionary's skeptical bishop declares, "The Virgin is not someone who schedules her appearances like a television show."

Indeed.

And faith without works is dead. The Works of Mercy are not a pre-recorded tape to be watched at my convenience. Fast-forward through the boring parts.

It's coffee-smelling time. Gotta quit counting sheep.

May all the one-armed mothers, the mothers with babies and the women who see them, in grottos and buses and bookstores have patience with me.

Grant us patience with each other as we labor, at night, giving birth to ourselves.

I used to tell
Shirley MacLaine jokes

I used to tell Betty Ford Center jokes.
Now I am one.
LINDA ELLERBEE

Another car whizzed down Yonge Street, packed to illegal proportions with World Series partiers. Somewhere, I imagined, more sober folks were discussing the morning's news.

I, however (cynic extraordinaire, being of soundproof mind and with know-it-all edge aforethought), was going to a New Age healing seminar at a bookstore that incorporated a pyramid in its logo.

At least, I would be if I could I squeeze my way through the Omega Centre to the seminar room at the back. The store was jammed with sandal-shod customers, most crowded around a

TV showing Disney cartoons. (A nearby poster proclaims: It's Never Too Late To Have A Happy Childhood!!)

If this sandalwood incense doesn't knock me over, I thought, then I'll lose my balance when this Tibetan meditation music collides with my inner ear...

Then stopped myself – before God sent me a toe-stubbing accident to shut me up. (Sure enough, I came within inches of colliding with a figurine display case. Would've served me right to pull a Glass Menagerie and have to take home a You-Break-It, You-Buy-It crystal unicorn with its horn knocked off.)

After all, *I* was here. These UFO enthusiasts might find my belief in, say, the Assumption, pretty ridiculous. Or not.

Jung was fascinated by the Assumption, and good old C. G. was well represented on the Omega's shelves, as were Merton, Nouwen, Teresa of Avila. A pocket-sized *The Way of a Pilgrim* was misshelved beside *Inner Balance through High Colonics*.

Victor Frankl, 12-Step stuff...Come on, Kath, you own half these books! Why the closed-minded carping?

Well, because New Agers strike working-class me as hopelessly yuppie. They talk Love and Peace, but also Prosperity and Longevity, and that contradictory, self-indulgent materialism sparks tornadoes in the trailer park of my soul. I read once that their precious talismanic crystals are actually imported from South Africa. Surely, I thought, New Agers will care about boycott-busting (not to mention "bad vibes"). Nope – they kept on buying the stupid things. So I swore off all things Aquarian.

That was before I got sick.

Because another New Age buzzword is Healing.

Still barely believing I'd entered a place in which ponytailed guys named Seth actually volunteer to realign your chakras, I followed my fellow bliss-ites into the seminar.

Many therapists ask their clients to use affirmations. Put simplistically, if you grew up being told, "You'll never amount to anything," then writing out "I am a worthwhile person" 20 times a day helps undo the harm. Call it positive brainwashing.

American author and cancer survivor Louise Hay believes affirmations can heal at a physical as well as emotional/psychological level. I was here to learn this technique.

I'd expected the ridiculous ("the left baby toe is the seat of divine wisdom" or something) but some was at least semi-sublime. I shared Hay's "attitudinal" rather than "symptomatic" approach. Her head-cold affirmation isn't "My nose is not stuffed up" but "I allow my mind to relax." People do seem to get colds just when life becomes too hectic (around exams, or when stuck in a dead-end job) and "official" summer vacation time is months away...

After the lecture proper, we were given small mirrors. Uh-oh. Theories were fun, but having to act on them? In front of people? That hostile, skeptical voice returned: "You're washing your brain in a New Age Laundromat!"

"This is a respected self-esteem exercise," the facilitator explained. "They do this at the Clarke Institute."

What a relief.

"Now, look in the mirror and repeat after me: 'I love myself.'"

Ugh.

Everyone, quietly, haltingly, obeyed.

Not me. Seeing my own lips moving, hearing my own voice, made me nauseated.

Next, same deal, no mirrors. We stood and said, "I am willing to change; I release old resentments." Even me. I refused, however, to close my eyes and raise my arms. I'd vowed upon entering Flakeland to avoid anything cult-like, and these gestures made visions of Kool-Aid and cyanide dance in my head.

I bought Hay's book despite its off-putting title *You Can Heal Your Life* and cutesy rainbow cover design. And despite our facilitator's predilection for sneezing fits, to which she succumbed throughout the seminar, and which were immune to all the affirmations she could muster.

That paradox characterizes my on-again, off-again affair with the New Age. My opinions about alternative medicine and metaphysics fluctuate from day to day, week to week, and often depend more on the behavior of New Age believers than on the beliefs themselves.

Pastimes and drugs, and features of the press

To communicate with Mars, converse with spirits,
To report the behaviour of the sea monster,
Describe the horoscope, haruspicate or scry,
Observe disease in signatures, evoke
Biography from the wrinkles of the palm
And tragedy from fingers;
...all these are usual
Pastimes and drugs, and features of the press:
And always will be, some of them especially
When there is distress of nations and perplexity
Whether on the shores of Asia,
or in the Edgware Road.
T. S. ELIOT, *THE DRY SALVAGES*, 1941

Peter Weller and Judy Davis don't know what they want to be when they grow up.

"So what?" you ask. Well, for one thing, they're over 40, not to mention white, well-educated and well past well-to-do.

"So what?" you ask again. Funny, that was my reaction exactly.

The New Age landed on a number of critics' Top Ten lists the year it came out. That drew the film to my attention, as did the movie's title and ad campaign, which seemed to promise a scathing little satire of trendy Californian metaphysics. Unfortunately, the one blow this film deals to mind-over-matter spirituality is this: all the affirmations one can muster won't magically make *The New Age* a better film.

How sad. Grinning gurus, prosperity prophets and men's movement Poo-Bahs are doubtlessly ripe for satirical picking. Or are they? Perhaps said folks are so inherently silly that mocking them is akin to gilding the granola...

Anyway, within the film's first two minutes, both Weller and Davis respond to mundane crises at their respective jobs by...quitting! In self-righteous huffs, no less. (Such an action is one of many yuppified luxuries I could never afford.)

And within the first five minutes, we hear the words "co-dependent," "visualization," and "journey." Such words let us know immediately just what kind of characters we're dealing with here, which is admirable. However, when using such words in a comedy, it's often advisable to attach them to actual jokes.

After consulting a guru at a cocktail party, Weller and Davis realize they're "only good at two things – talking and shopping." They open a rarefied boutique called The Hipocracy – the "hip aristocracy," you see. The couple try to white-knuckle their way to wealth and happiness using (albeit haphazardly) New Age methods instead of economic theories.

Is the shop a success? I doubt most viewers will even care. I still remember walking into *The Big Chill* determined to dislike its Woodstock-refugee characters, sight unseen – and walking out impressed by that film's surprisingly literate screenplay and fine ensemble cast. Where *The Big Chill* succeeds, *The New Age* fails: not for a moment did I catch a glimpse of humor or humanity. Or humility.

At one point (while lounging beside the pool) Davis asks rhetorically, "Why are we so awful?"

People like her are "so awful" because they'd been led to believe they'd share, or even surpass, their parents' postwar prosperity; because they mistake "spirituality" for "witchcraft," with the sorts of naive, self-serving rituals that children would no doubt concoct if left to their own devices; because, contrary to its adherents' protestations, there *is* something "new" about "the New Age": for the first time in history, "spirituality" has been divorced from altruism and sacrifice.

Meanwhile, back on planet Earth, many people tossed on the New Age compost heap are voicing their protests. M. Scott Peck takes pains to remind his rabid fans that the first line of his mega-seller *The Road Less Traveled* is, "Life is difficult." I recently heard John "Inner Child" Bradshaw mock a popular New Age poster by fairly shouting, "Ladies and gentlemen, it IS too late to have a happy childhood!" And 12-Step programs have taken to calling themselves "mutual-help" (as opposed to "self-help") groups.

As usual, the death knell's been sounded surest by a poet – namely, Jane Miller – who recently wrote,

The twentieth century, begun in Vienna,
has ended in California.

I do hope "ended" is the operative word, but I'm obliged to believe both Eliot and Jesus: the poor of spirit will always be with us. I include myself among them, and am frequently tempted by wishful thinking and easy answers. I am, however, increasingly convinced that living well requires fewer "deep thoughts" and more simple acts.

The dark night
of the body

Much ado about nada

If he is completely inexperienced he will get the idea
that he is very holy
because of all the holy feelings that are
teeming in his heart.
All these things mean very little or nothing at all...
and there is only an accidental difference
between them
and the tears that children sometimes shed
when they go to the movies.

THOMAS MERTON, *NEW SEEDS OF CONTEMPLATION*

I attend the monthly Healing Service at Toronto's Our Lady
of Lourdes parish. This Mass and Anointing of the Sick is for
people with HIV/AIDS, but everyone is, most emphatically,
welcome.

I look forward to this service all month, to seeing my friends, to the anointing itself. But I wonder why, after all this time, I can't describe this made-to-order event in my column.

I simply have nothing to say.

More Merton:

The mind finds itself entering uneasily
into the shadows of a strange and silent night...
It tries to force acts of thought and will.
Sometimes it makes a mad effort to squeeze some
feeling of fervor out of itself
which is, incidentally,
the worst thing it could possibly do.

More nothing.

I undergo a session of therapeutic touch, a modern variation of "laying on of hands." The intelligent, down-to-earth nurse practitioner inspires my confidence; I'm completely at ease and not at all skeptical as she "reads my energy field" and gently rests her hands on my arms and legs.

"People often react emotionally to this therapy," she says. "Let me know what feelings come up."

Nothing. I check myself out for "healing sensations" (whatever they are). Other than a tingling in my left arm, I don't feel anything, either physically or emotionally.

There is, however, a sty in my mind's eye – a peculiar, persistent mental image which lasts throughout the session.

I'm not what you'd call a "Mary person," so I'm surprised that my thoughts are of her, or rather a statue of her – the once-painted, now bleached-to-bone white variety, the sort quite clearly subjected to a post-Vatican II turpentine bath. Not the type of statue I particularly care for.

But I'm too puzzled and embarrassed by this unusual *idée fixe* to share it with the nurse.

...many of those who seem to be so superior to the sensible element in religion show,
by their devotions, their taste for sentimental pictures and sticky music and mushy spiritual reading,
that their whole interior life is a concentrated campaign for "lights" and "consolations" and "tears of compunction," if not "interior words"
with, perhaps, the faintly disguised hope of a vision or two and, eventually, the stigmata.

"Anyone can practice therapeutic touch," the nurse assures me. "Put your palms together. Now move them back and forth until you feel the energy."

I give it a try.

"Feel it?" she asks.

My face turns red. I feel a panic coming on.

"Nope," I reply. Nothing. Again.

"Don't worry," she says. "That's how I was when I started. Keep practicing..."

I walk home, faintly disappointed. Just as I always did from the Lourdes Mass. I'd wanted more. More what? Euphoria. Excitement. A dramatic, revival-tent, snake-handling, tongue-speaking healing. Not nothing.

But what did I expect? My invisible disease doesn't impair my senses, and now drugs keep my arthritis away. If these healing measures had "taken," how would I even know?

I blush again remembering my inability to "do" therapeutic touch myself, to feel my own "vibes" for goodness sake, let alone the nurse's. I hate failing, had secretly hoped the nurse would take one look at my aura and dub me The Next Great Healer.

I'd envied her obvious compassion, her (let's face it) really cool job, and had begun to entertain fantasies of myself skipping along, healing people left and right with a wave of my hand. So much for that.

Strolling through the nurse's neighborbood on the way to my own, I feel compelled to go into St. Patrick's church, which I've passed many times but never entered. The place is deserted.

I tiptoe self-consciously to the front of the church where, to the right of the altar, I spot "my" very white statue of Mary...

✣ ✣ ✣

My encounter with that statue in St. Patrick's church didn't spark some pyrotechnical mystical experience. I just sat there for a while, lit a candle, and left.

Nada.

Or not.

I did get the idea, in that empty church, that perhaps I should write about Nothing. And turned for inspiration to that great Stylist of Zilch, Thomas Merton.

Specifically, *New Seeds of Contemplation* – Merton at his cranky, scolding best (or worst, depending on what day you ask me). My copy, now several years old, has miraculously survived countless violent flings across my room. I defy Stephen King to write anything as terrifying as Merton's scathing essay on "what faith is not," which would compel even the most self-confident readers to surreptitiously sniff their own spiritual armpits.

As uncomfortable as *New Seeds* made me (again), I continued to read it because the stages of prayer Merton described reminded me of similar stages of chronic illness: periods of consolation and desolation, of relapse and wellness.

"I feel simply wretched," he muttered.
And suddenly he was moved
by an extraordinary and extravagant thrill of joy
and suspense,
of which he was so conscious that he sat motionless
waiting for it to come again.
It did not – only the misery remained.

THOMAS MANN, *THE MAGIC MOUNTAIN*

Ireland's patron saint seemed to be following me. As I walked from St. Patrick's church to the St. Patrick subway stop, every bar along the way advertised their upcoming March 17 celebrations. I remembered, to my shame, last St. Patrick's Day: depressed, exhausted, in excruciating pain, I'd decided I needed "cheering up"; consuming quantities of green food coloring far above the legal limit was actually the least embarrassing stunt I pulled that horrible night. I'm often amazed I have any friends left.

As I continued walking to the subway (wishing medical science would perfect the selective lobotomy) I tried to think of happier times. A few months after that disastrous St. Patrick's Day, I had finally taken a drug that worked. My arthritis disappeared overnight. I had been elated, energetic, in love with life.

But the prednisone honeymoon was over. As my drug dosage was reduced, my energy decreased. The novelty of being able to button my clothes again had worn off months ago. Lupus had always been an adventure, first agonizing, then thrilling – not to mention something new to write about. Now life was once again...ordinary.

Like a contemplative novice, I view this turn of events with some alarm. No matter how many books about chronic illness assure me that these ups and downs are, however frustrating, typical and unavoidable, I can't quite release my need for last summer's exciting rush of "consolation."

Yesterday upon the stair
I met a man who wasn't there.
He wasn't there again today –
I wish that man would go away.

I sometimes even miss my pain. Not quite "miss" – but its absence is tangible, an amputee's phantom limb. It has to come back some day; such is the nature of chronic illness. So I wonder where it's got to, probe that absence as a child tongues the hole where a tooth used to be. I don't care for this "cloud of unknowing," sleeping, as it were, with one eye open, ears pricked for the sound of a break-in.

Am I such a product of my sensation-crazed society that I'm rushing from the Healing Mass to therapeutic touch to who knows what, desperately trying to relieve this feeling of ordinary, tepid wellness that I can't help calling "boredom"?

What does healing feel like?

They will see that
in this apparently dark and frustrated condition
they are readjusting themselves, they are being
peacefully and gently purified
of false hopes and illusory conceptions,
and they are being made ready
for the journey in the desert which,
after many privations,
leads at last to the Promised Land.

THOMAS MERTON, *NEW SEEDS OF CONTEMPLATION*

A Lenten notebook

Radiation meditation

When pain needs rest
it lies down in the bones
and dreams up fresh surprises, o its repertoire of style
exceeds New York.

Don McKay, *Nostra*

My back's grown a strange new pain. "Strange" as in "sudden, unexpected"; I've been fairly pain-free for months.

A strange location too. Not hard work's commonplace, lower-back ache, but one stretched across my shoulder blades.

Perhaps I'm sprouting wings...

Mostly we are tuned to the heart (passion, drugs, intrigues, attacks), but it is through the bone self that the deaf hear symphonies, that mothers know beforehand that their children are in trouble, and that we

maintain our slender diplomatic ties with the future and
the dead. Bones attend to deep earth, while your heart
is learning, year by year, to listen to your watch.

DON MCKAY, *BONE POEMS*

I speculate with my doctor on the pain's possible cause. Stress?
Winter?

We're reducing my prednisone by five milligram incre-
ments every six weeks. A gentle coaxing. No short sharp shocks
to my adrenal glands allowed.

And my bloodwork is "outstanding," my strength improves
each week.

But I know that as the drugs "go down" the pain "goes
up," comes back. "Back..."

As the doctor probes my spine, my brain's darned poetry
cells (can't live with 'em, can't kill 'em) tie their simile shoes,
take a meditative walk:

"Here's Johnny!" drawls the pain – Jack Nicholson in *The
Shining*, the maniac I just imagined I'd escaped from while I
hid in my cortisone closet. But he's tracked me down, my back's
the door, his axe cracks through, its blade like the two sharp
bony ones I own, the bones in which my current troubles live.
Jack's eye glistens, giggles even, through a slit in the splintered
door. "Daddy's home..."

(Get behind me Satan.)

The doctor's voice hits my brain's pause button.
"I'd like to send you for X-rays."

Now we know the price of X-ray:
if you want to see your bones you have to
flirt with death a little. Moon-bathe.
Anticipate their liberation from your flesh.

Once upon a time
shoe stores had a peepshow that could
melt your skin and show the bones
inside your feet (plenty of room for him to grow there,
ma'am).
You looked down zillions, back
into an ocean where a loose
family of fish was
wriggling in blue spooky light

There are other worlds.
Your dead dog swims in the earth.
Don McKay, *Bone Poems*

Downstairs in radiology, I wait for my name to be called.
    "We probably won't see any problems until we go down to
15 mg," my doctor had said once. And I'm still on 25.

Pulling out my datebook, I calculate my drug reduction schedule. Down to 20 mg on January 15. Down to 15 mg just after Ash Wednesday.

And down to 10 mg (if we make it that far; may hit some turbulence, have to fly back up) on Good Friday.

Highly amusing. Like so many things about lupus. Like the fact that, although I don't have cancer, I take an anti-cancer medication that (according to The Canadian Drug Guide) "may cause cancer."

I ponder these puns and paradoxes in my heart, words on words, meditation as opposed to contemplation.

But I can't, for some reason, find the humor in X-rays today, am uncharacteristically anxious as I sit here. Bloodtests, EMGs don't faze me anymore. And this is hardly chemo, dialysis.

Just a routine, radioactive unwrapping of my insides.

Some words rise up:

The Kingdom of God is within you.

Yuck.

Those words made Tolstoy go ballistic, but I hate them.

Why would God want to live inside of messy, bloody, all-too-human me, within this unhealthy, betrayal-prone body, with its Iscariot immune system?

I have no problem with (sometimes prefer) the childish notion of God-in-the-sky. Up there somewhere. Not inside my soon-to-be-revealed-through-the-wonders-of modern-technology bones.

Someone calls my name.

God is in the midst of her,
she shall not be moved;...
PSALM 46:5 (RSV)

"Please to put on a gown."

The technician directs me to a changing-stall just off the x-ray room proper.

Great. I pull off my sweater, feel that now-familiar tug at my back. No, not the pain, though that makes undressing difficult.

I mean the itch of clothes against skin which reminds me that, thanks to steroids, dark stripes of truly unattractive black fuzz have grown across my shoulders, down my spine.

(Hey, kids! Ideas For Lent: Grow Your Own Hairshirt!)

And now this x-ray guy will see it through this back-lacing hospital gown.

Entering the cool, dark x-ray room, I'm unimpressed by the obviously Korean War-issue machine poised to take my picture.

"Please lie down."

I'm twisted into a presumably more photogenic shape, arms up, legs just so, increasing the pain we're supposed to be exploring.

"Good. Now, please to lie very still." His footsteps patter off.

(If this is so safe, how come you're hiding way over there?)

"Very still please."

Concentrate, girl. On that spot on the wall. Grab some words so you won't move.

Be still and know that I am God.

(The contemplative rallying cry, as I recalled from my reading, from my practice, years ago. Had "done" contemplation, but felt moved...)

"No please. Very still!"

(...back to words. Or moved myself. Out of fear? That vulnerable emptiness, that stripping away. Like now.)

The heathen raged, the kingdoms were moved: he uttered his voice, the earth melted.

BUZZZZZZ: the machine takes my picture.

(Melts my flesh. Radiation does that in more ways than one.)

"Other side now please."

The Lord of hosts is with us; the God of Jacob is our refuge. Selah.

("Host" means "army." "Angel." "Daddy, teacher says, every time a bell rings...")

BUZZZZZ.

(Almost forgot about those wings I might be growing. My spine and its ladder of ribs. And yeah, I know, *selah* is just...)

"Still please."

(...an ancient stage direction).

BUZZZZ.

The photo-shoot is over, I change my clothes, grab my purse to leave.

"No, wait!" The technician beckons me back. "Sit. Wait. Wait and see."

A few moments later, he pulls out the X-rays, holds them up before my eyes.

"See? You! And you. Inside, see?"

(Okay, Okay. Yuck.)

These grey pictures. Hate to see myself reduced to ash like that.

There's no sign of God, let alone wing-sprouts.

It's rather hard to work just now.
I am at the moment when one feels the reaction.
After five doses of X-rays,
one is hotted up inside like a furnace
and one's very bones seem to be melting.
I suppose this is the moment
when real martyrs break into song.

KATHERINE MANSFIELD

A few weeks later I'm back at Wellesley Hospital, this time for the monthly meeting of the Lupus Support Group. I'm the only hardcore regular. The ever-changing patients on Rheumatology sometimes come – wheelchairs, IVs and all. But women from "the outside," often just diagnosed, tend to show up once, cry a little, take pamphlets, never return.

I rather like having a captive audience for my jokes. The others seem to find throwing light on their problems, sharing their fears, more embarrassing than therapeutic: we silently stare at our shoes after someone's spoken tearfully of her husband's refusal to help with housework, or his disgust at her weight gain due to prednisone. I know I talk too much at times because I don't want to listen.

To hear about fear of disability and divorce. Of going on welfare or having it taken away. So far two women have explained that their relatives don't believe they have a "real" disease: their languages have no word for "lupus."

The word of God is something alive and active:
it cuts like any double-edged sword but more finely;
it can slip through the place where the soul is divided
from the spirit,
or joints from the marrow...
HEBREWS 4:12

"If you don't hear anything in a week..." No one ever calls me about my X-rays. In the wacky world of medicine, no news is good news. I guess they didn't show anything.

It can judge the secret emotions and thoughts.
No created thing can hide from him; everything is
uncovered and open
to the eyes of the one to whom we must give an
account of ourselves.
HEBREWS 4:12–13

X-rays usually reveal brokenness. What did mine show?
If God's word is a sword, what is silence?
How does that song go again? If your phone don't ring, it'll be me...

...everything exposed by the light becomes visible,
for everything that becomes visible is light.
Therefore it is said, "Sleeper, awake!
Rise from the dead,
and Christ will shine on you."
EPHESIANS 5:13–14

No wonder I find these meetings easy and fun: I may talk a lot, but I never actually say anything important. When I feel pretty good, which is much of the time, I smugly show that off.

But I rarely discuss my bad days. I don't want to look inside myself, acknowledge my problems, let alone expose them to the light of day.

I want to forget that I was one of those vulnerable, confused, weeping women once too, not that long ago.

So much that refuses to be written or
unwritten, won't
make up your mind. That
moment in the life of every headache
when lucidity approaches
and withdraws: fine points
stand within your vision but
outside your grasp, declining to visit
or rent the attic.

DON MCKAY, *NOSTRA*

I have a headache while I write this. That phantom back pain disappeared, but yesterday I threw up. A new lupus experience, probably a drug side effect. Never a dull moment. What next? A woman in my support group is having neurological problems. The other day she was eating some fruit when the phone rang; she lifted a banana to her ear and said, "Hello."

My train of thought derailed a few miles back. Something about X-rays and Lent.

Lupus is a lifelong Lent, a chronic opportunity for self-examination, do-it-yourself X-rays. For lying still as Isaac on the table, under the dangerous camera; a Pompeii baby, turned to stone, ashes to ashes, a fossil waiting to be dug up, dusted off, examined.

Lent, a listening time. Can only knit my hands together, a child's earnest First Communion pose. This is the church, this is the steeple. So tight the bones show through, fasting fingers, white-knuckling the rollercoaster ride: mouth shut, teeth clenched against the scream.

Lent, waiting room of waiting rooms. Hold your own hand. Wait for your name to be called.

Those not-so-spiritual exercises

I hate physiotherapy.

Writers are notorious for concocting creative ways to avoid writing. Walk that dog. Brew that coffee. Re-alphabetize that card catalogue index of rare *Brady Bunch* memorabilia.

How much does this particular scribe despise her 10-minute regimen of leg-lifts and stretches? She's writing this just to avoid it.

I hate exercises, period. Although before I got sick, I'd joined the Y. Until then, my idea of a good cardiovascular work-out was wrenching the pop-top off a Coke can, and I thought

The Nautilus was some legendary German U-boat. I said I was exercising to "get healthy," but secretly I just wanted to transform myself into Rebecca DeMornay so Leonard Cohen would mistake me for the real Rebecca DeMornay and take *me* to the Oscars instead.

Months later, too sick to "four-more, three-more" anymore, I admitted I'd never liked aerobics class anyway. So contrived and artificial. Imagine what spying aliens report back to their planets:

"Commander Pin-Doof, these humans are a strange species. A century ago, they tilled the land and toiled in steel mills. Today they pay bumpy men large sums of cash to scream at them while they jump up and down in bad outfits. Remember that toxic waste we dumped here in the '70s? They dance to it!"

Even the food at the Y was weird. Why would people trying to burn off cellulite eat nothing but the only two foods in the universe – egg salad and cottage cheese – that look exactly like it?

Robin Williams says cocaine is God's way of telling you you have too much money. Maybe lupus was God's way of telling me to finally decide what I wanted, and needed, to do with my life. Being sick was just the excuse I needed to stop trying to be a *Cosmo* Girl.

(Okay, so my friends are laughing really hard right now, especially those who've seen the Tina Turner quotation on my bathroom mirror: "I live like a monk. A monk with red lips, short dresses and big hair.")

So I thought lupus was my ticket to a land without exercise, a good-for-eternity Note To The Gym Teacher. Wrong. I was assigned an Arthritis Society physiotherapist when I left the hospital, and since then, I've been (reluctantly) doing the exercises she taught me.

Physiotherapy is the only part of my daily routine that reminds me I'm a "sick person." Lying on my bed in the middle of the day, verrry sloooowly lifting my legs up and down...I feel like the invalid I am.

Musical accompaniment doesn't help, in spite of John Callahan's example. Callahan's the world's only recovering alcoholic quadriplegic cartoonist. When John and his attendant do his physio, he sings (to the tune of *Locomotion*) "Come on baby! Do the Range-of-Motion!"

I tried praying though. When I worked up to 10 repetitions of my five assigned exercises, I tried squeezing a rosary into the routine. But the resulting garble ("Hail Mary full of lift two three four") wouldn't have converted Richmond Hill, let alone Russia.

My therapist told me, rather sadly, that most of her clients don't do their exercises (and then wonder why they don't get better). I force myself to continue my physiotherapy because it works. I can climb stairs again, and my thighs have lost their resemblance to warped violins.

GOD RIDES A YAMAHA

They still aren't Rebecca DeMornay's thighs, but I'll be wearing an evening gown anyway, so I don't think Leonard will notice.

Where the clocks, and the people, don't work

A Monday morning in January. Sub-zero. Six inches of snow. Not the day I'd have chosen for my first annual Disability interview.

I cursed (under my breath) as I slipped along unshoveled Parliament Street. At the taunting, wobbling panhandlers (still celebrating New Year's?) encamped, like a stranded Arctic expedition, at the corner of Gerrard. And (aloud) at the speeding car that grazed the stroller being pushed by the bundled-up mother beside me as we were all about to cross that street.

When I arrived at the Family Benefits office, I shoved my papers to a harried worker through a slot in the bulletproof glass. It was 9:50, but the clock that hung behind her read 11:47, and remained in that state of *karma*-breeding *maya* for the duration of my visit.

The other waiting clients seemed just as broken. One longhaired, tattooed man knocked persistently on the glass partition, demanding an immediate replacement for a lost cheque. Refusing to believe that cheques weren't printed on the premises, he just kept spelling out his name, letter by letter, and rattling off his Social Insurance and caseload numbers, as if they were a mystical lock combination, or magic spell which, if recited often enough, would grant him his impossible wish.

The rest of us were mute, save for the odd sniffle. The downcast crowd, with their makeshift vinyl winterwear and mismatched mittens, and casts and canes, resembled a none-too-successful junior hockey team, waiting for the bus back to Orillia, or wherever home was.

Bus terminals are terminally pathetic, but at least they have coffee and donuts. And clocks that work. And the promise of eventual departure.

Don't get me wrong: I'm grateful to live in Canada, where a doctor I didn't pay convinced a government I didn't vote for to give me money for doing nothing more spectacular or productive than just getting well.

And I hate it. I hated that office. And as ashamed as I am to admit it, most of all I hated the shabby, beaten-down clients.

And myself. Because that morning I was, by implication, "one of them."

I suppose I always have been, having lived below the poverty line much of my life – a fact which shocked my hardworking mom and me when the "Single Mother With Child" level was announced one night on the news. After all, we'd lived on far less for years. I was 19 then, and equally amazed a few months later, when my college loans officer asked if my mother had "left out a digit" in the form-box marked "Income." I'd never thought I was poor.

And I thought of my colleagues at *Catholic New Times*, just a few blocks south of the Disability Office. When they'd hired me, years ago, they'd practically apologized about the modest salary. Why? Given my lifelong frugality, it was more money than I knew how to spend – even in high-priced Toronto. I still didn't think I was poor.

And still didn't, when I laid out those *CNT* articles about "solidarity with the poor." To me, that meant just about anything...except being actually poor.

What gets me now isn't my income (interestingly, it's virtually the same as my old *CNT* salary). It's that today, I have a worker instead of being one.

This isn't what I wanted to do when I grew up: showing my bankbook to a total stranger under the staring eye of a stupid broken clock.

More importantly, this isn't who I wanted to be. I'd gone to all the right rallies and read all the right books.

And had turned into just another loser with a superiority complex, with more compunction than compassion.

When my interview was over, I hoped for a sudden *deus ex machina*, a lightning-flash vision that would reveal, through my tears, Christ in the faces of the frozen, unblinking clients I was leaving behind. But instead of God's voice, the only sound was the scratchy bellow of another client's name being mispronounced over the loudspeaker. And all I saw and felt and smelled was fear and disgust.

I wanted to run all the way back to my flat, but the snow was too deep and my home was too far.

How to be sick, unemployed, and insane

1. Wake Up. Are you in pain? If "yes," roll over (if you can) and go back to sleep. If "no," roll over (since you can) and go back to sleep.

2. Really Wake Up. Drink the first of today's 16 coffees, preferably from a mug emblazoned with an amusing slogan. Mine says "Naturally Blonde: Please Speak Slowly." This mug assures visiting social workers and concerned family and friends that you are Keeping Your Sense Of Humor.

3.   Keep Your Sense Of Humor

a)   Stop Reading or Watching the News. The news, like modern jazz or bridal showers, is something most people only pretend to enjoy. Read supermarket tabloids instead. Their lies are more entertaining than those in *The Globe and Mail*, and they at least mention God more often, especially when His Face appears in a puddle of diesel fuel located just north of Scranton, Pennsylvania.

While others were reading about the Quebec referendum and the World Series, I, through the tabloids, was following The Year's Real Story: country singer Naomi Judd's miraculous cure from hepatitis-C, which she claims occurred when she touched the face of Billy Graham on her 18-inch Panasonic. An inspiration, if ever there was one, to

b)   Watch More TV. Algebra does have real-world applications. *Roseanne* is now syndicated five times a day; decipher the viewing schedule so you'll never see the same episode twice. For *Star Trek: The Next Generation*, try logarithms.

Now when someone at a dinner party mentions "the war between Chad and Libya," you'll think they're referring to two characters on *Street Legal*. Everyone will laugh, further evidence that you're Keeping Your Sense Of Humor.

4.   Go To Dinner Parties. (Free food.)

5.   Do Volunteer Work/Take Up A Hobby. I collect Signs Of The Coming Apocalypse. After performing Steps 3a/b, I leave ominous newsbites on my (employed) friends' answering machines so they'll be forewarned of the approaching conflagration. Real-life Signs Of The Coming Apocalypse include the L.A. riots, the Westray mine disaster, and the fact that Leonard Cohen quit smoking.

   So now you too can recognize The End Of The World, which sometimes bears a striking resemblance to

6.   Three In The Afternoon. "Three in the afternoon is too early to do most things and too late to do anything else." That's the most intelligent, let alone intelligible, sentence Jean-Paul Sartre ever uttered, with the possible exception of his last words, which were, reportedly, "Maybe I'll just die now and stop bugging everyone."

   You may feel this way at Three In The Afternoon, the only time *Roseanne* isn't on, not to mention *Star Trek: The Next Generation*. But fear not! There's something worth living for, something coming up just one hour from now, and that something is

7. *Oprah.* Oprahoprahoprah! Oprah for President! Oprah for Secretary General of the UN! "Oprah" spelled backwards is "Harpo," surely a fact of major mystical significance. Perhaps the Apocalypse has been postponed. You tune in and – yes! – incredibly, Oprah's guest today is...Roseanne! You call your friends with the glorious news that they can flush their cyanide pills down the toilet.

   Rumor has it Oprah's getting married. You dream of attending the bridal shower, which you will only pretend to enjoy. Although the food will be free, unlike your

8. Dinner. Kraft. Yum. And don't forget to take your

9. Medication. Contemplate the cortisone-induced black hairs growing in swirling crop-circle formations across your chest. Call the supermarket tabloids to report this phenomenon. Ask them, when they next see Him, to mention it to God.

Hey! (Hey!) You! (You!)
Get off of my cloud! or

How to cheat death
and influence people

In *Prayer*, Richard Foster observes that, "the contemplation of one's own death is among the most time-honored approaches to personal transformation."

And I thought I was just cultivating morbid self-pity when I'd wondered whether death would be preferable to a lifetime of chronic pain and/or another week of hospital food.

Pondering my own demise is nothing new. Like any good Catholic, my happy moods consist of being cheerful for ten minutes, then wondering what make of car I'm about to be hit by.

If lupus or a '57 Chevy don't get me first, I expect to die of cigarette-related causes: specifically, breaking my neck after tripping over my welcome mat when I open the door for the pizza I sent for at two in the morning in order to get some cigarettes.

Heaven: what's it really like? Is it (as our parents told us during thunderstorms) really God's bowling alley? And if so, do we have to rent shoes?

Some claim to know. They've had Near-Death Experiences (NDEs) which, as the name implies, are similar to equally scary phenomena like High School Dances (HSDs) (betcha wondered why the last song is always *Stairway To Heaven*) and Babysitting Three-Year-Old Twins On New Year's Eve (B3x2/TOOT).

During an NDE, you allegedly travel down a tunnel toward a light, and then deceased friends and relatives greet you.

This scenario poses some problems for me. One: an embarrassing lack of dead relatives. (The women in my family don't die – they just shop less frequently.)

Hence Problem Two: my genetically-inherited, stubborn refusal to "pass on."

God and I have discussed this problem and agreed it's going to take someone truly remarkable to convince me to, as they say, "go towards the light." There's only one man for the job, and that man is Robert Francis Kennedy who, besides being The Cutest Guy Who Ever Lived, was also really gorgeous and totally cute.

What God doesn't know is that I plan to use this arrangement to very cleverly cheat death. Here's the scam:

My instinctive reaction to actually meeting, in person, the very wonderful Robert Francis Kennedy will be, quite naturally, to scream my head clean off.

Now, Screaming In Heaven must be "A Bad Thing To Do," right up there with Being An Announcer For Public Television Pledge Drives and Not Just Wearing Old Spice Aftershave But Buying It For Someone As An Actual Gift.

Screaming In Heaven will, I believe, constitute a big enough breach of celestial etiquette to get me kicked out of there faster than you can say "Elisabeth Kübler-Ross."

In this way, I could bounce back and forth between life and death forever, but don't really want to. God and I are still ironing out our "heaven issues," but I have extracted a promise that there'll be a not-too-smelly pair of size fives waiting at the shoe rental counter when I get there.

2

God
and the
single
girl

St. Anselm's proof for the existence of Robert Redford

Ah, spring! And with spring, a Young Human Being Person's fancy turns to...*Indecent Proposal.*

I'm getting old; that is, I've become The Thing I Most Despise. Specifically, I've been, quite suddenly and without my consent, transformed into One Of Those Idiots Who Criticizes Movies They Haven't Even Seen. I'll console myself with Mark Twain's words, "You don't have to eat the egg to know it's rotten" and proceed regardless.

Indecent Proposal asks: Would you sleep with Robert Redford for a million dollars?

As I'm sure you've guessed from that brief synopsis, *Indecent Proposal* is another distinguished example of American Cinema, right up there with *Chopper Chicks in Zombie Town*. (Actually, I liked *Chopper Chicks*, but then my favorite director is John Waters, a man who wears Kleenex boxes for bedroom slippers.)

I refuse even to see this movie for a million dollars; as the trailers alone attest, *Indecent Proposal* just plain stinks. (Critic Liz Braun advised, "Wait till it comes out on video, then use it as a doorstop.") But the ethical questions raised by the film have captured the American imagination (admittedly a rather dubious accomplishment, requiring as it does only a very small trap). Talk shows are featuring *Indecent Proposal*'s controversial moral dilemma. It's true: while multitudes of angels dance, forgotten and uncounted, on pinheads everywhere, people are debating instead the relative merits of celebrity prostitution.

I surveyed my friends, who are, admittedly, not at all representative of the general population, unless the words "general population" can somehow be stretched to include "unemployed circus freaks." Heck, some of them liked *Chopper Chicks* even more than I did. The results of this survey are accurate within three to five percentage points of alcohol.

Jane: (derisive snorting noise).

Frank: (derisive snorting noise picked up from Jane).

Yvonne: (unprintable).

Daryl: "What did Yvonne say?"

There you have it: the philosophical insights of Young People Today, some of whom are the products of a solid Catholic education which, besides giving them the ability to reason and debate in the great scholastic tradition, also taught them how to sell huge quantities of overpriced chocolate-covered almonds.

I'm surprised I've caught the *Indecent Proposal* bug. Come on: Robert Redford wouldn't ask me for directions to the nearest post office and I've never been mistaken for his co-star Demi Moore. Especially not since I began taking prednisone, which "may cause weight gain and unwanted hair growth." May? I've bubbled from a size three to a nine, and look like a character from *The Wind in the Willows*.

Ironically, the very thing – an incurable disease – which makes me the unlikely object of an "indecent proposal" from Robert Redford (or, for that matter, from Bozo the Clown), is also the very thing which makes me a deserving recipient of that aforementioned million dollars. After all, if I were unlucky enough to be sick and American, I'd need that much money just to survive. Another woman with lupus told me that, during a trip to the U.S., she went in for blood tests. Two minutes and four vials of blood later, she received a bill for (please extinguish your cigarettes) $1,600!! For a while, I was having 12 vials taken every two weeks.

So, "indecent proposals" – be they real or cinematic – are moot, academic, and other big words. The rites of spring are wrong for me. Few men really want to go out with the chronically ill, or know how to handle it when they do. (One date asked me, once too often, if I was "absolutely sure" that lupus wasn't contagious. "I was just asking," he muttered. "You were just leaving," I answered.)

I asked my friends what they thought of all this, and they said (collective derisive snort), "But, Kathy, we love you."

And I said, "Yeah, but you aren't Robert Redford."

No wonder that it's Mary that we love

Snow White stinks.

Watching that Disney movie when I was a kid, I wondered just why those perfectly able- (albeit tiny-) bodied dwarves required unpaid domestic help.

While pasty-faced Snow White warbled, "I'm wishing for the one I love to find me someday," I was wishing she'd either find a real job or else keel over into that well and thus bring to a merciful end her years of thankless, indentured servitude.

Sleeping Beauty? You mean "Narcoleptic and Necrophile Live Happily Ever After"? Ugh.

I loathe Disney's predilection for transforming sexy, violent, grim (pun intended) fairy tales into saccharine, sing-along shadows of their former selves.

Disney's so-called heroines are a particular peeve; even recent "liberated" ones disappoint. The Little Mermaid and the Beast's Belle are as big-eyed, long-haired, sweet-voiced and helplessly helpful as their animated ancestors.

Will Disney ever produce a truly radical reading of *Beauty and the Beast* – in which the Beast is a girl, and some nice guy loves her anyway?

(Until then, we're stuck with the original version – and with the "interesting" statistic that 9 out of 10 women stay with alcoholic husbands, and 9 out of 10 men leave alcoholic wives.)

101 Dalmations was pretty good. You can keep those yappy dogs, though – with her fabulous furs, bad make-up and nicotine fits, Cruella D'Evil is one of my heroines.

And then there's Mary Poppins.

People mis-remember Mary as a sappy goody-two-shoes, but's she's actually capable, fun-loving, and strong-willed – self-confident, and with good reason.

In short, Mary Poppins is the best female role-model in Disney's canon.

Mary literally blows the competition away. (Remember those sour, funereal nannies soaring off in a gust of wind?)

And who can forget Mary's job interview with Mr. Banks, in which she interviews him, and tables her salary expectations right off the bat!

Work it, girl!

Mary Poppins is ultimately about independence and individuality. Burt the Chimney Sweep sings, "I do what I like and I like what I do"; Mrs. Banks is a dedicated suffragist; the servants aren't servile; the children are willful...

Yes, amazingly, *Mary Poppins* is a wimp-free film. Even when Burt gently chides Mr. Banks for caring more about work than family, his speech doesn't sound like a snatch of sharing at a Men's Movement meeting.

And eventually Banks realizes that any authority he's wielded over the family was tenuous, based on brisk platitudes and benign neglect. He earns the children's love and respect only when he adopts Mary's sense of sensible whimsy.

Having accomplished her task to perfection (as usual) Mary dutifully, gracefully flies off to another job – not, thankfully, into Burt's arms (see "wimp-free" above).

Not bad for a movie set in 1910 and filmed in 1964.

I remember this film fondly, and not just because I admire Mary. During commercials, my Scottish grandmother delighted ten-year-old me with tales of real chimney sweeps and birdladies – and converted all the currency discussed in the movie into "real" money (see "Scottish" above).

And all right, I'll admit it: I just adore those little dancing penguins.

See! I'm not really such a Grinch. It's just that, as Mary Poppins says,

"Practically perfect people never permit sentiment to muddle their thinking."

No wonder that it's Mary that we love.

A transcendental meditation

I'm powerless over popular culture. I dog fresh fads and fashions like a bloodhound, scan the daily paper's "Entertainment" section and then recycle the remainder with nary a blush.

That's why I'm surprised by my knee-jerk distaste for so many current trends in matters theological.

For instance, I happen to *like* referring to God as my Father, thank you very much, for precisely the same reason many people don't: I've endured two of the mortal variety, and can honestly say that God is the only father I've ever had who's never let me down.

Then there was that retreat I once attended.

The facilitator asked the 30 of us if we preferred a transcendent notion of God to an immanent one. At the word "immanent," 29 hands shot obediently up to the sky.

("Up to the sky," hmmm? Interesting.)

Only my hand remained still. I'm usually half the age of the other participants at such events, so one might reasonably expect that I of all people would be receptive to the latest ideas. Nope. I suspect it's precisely due to my status as a "Vatican II baby" that I'm more embarrassed than inspired by lumbering liturgical dance and ersatz indigenous drumming.

One is, after all, inclined to rebel against one's upbringing, whatever its trappings. I do so envy pre-concilors, those lucky ducks who got to mutiny against Limbo and Latin; folk masses, felt-appliqué banners, those Casper-The-Friendly-Ghost illustrations in *Good News for Modern Man* – these hardly inspire the aspiring satirist. But I digress.

That retreat proved to be a life-altering experience indeed, although surely not in the manner the facilitators intended. I was granted a revelatory vision of my essential at-two-ness with the progressive Catholic universe, caught a glimpse of my Inner Old Fart.

Fortunately, I soon discovered concrete, if unlikely, proof that I wasn't quite alone – a "Deep Thoughts" greeting card of all things, which read:

If God is inside us
like some people say,
He'd better like burritos
'cause that's what he's getting.

Exactly! Immanence is so, well, unseemly. Like a squeamish schoolgirl with a horror of cooties, I've never outgrown the ghastly misconception that God will smother under last night's hastily-gobbled tub of Chocolate-Chocolate-Chip, or choke on my second-hand smoke.

And, poetically speaking, you must admit that transcendence is infinitely more majestic – unless you happen to be one of those poor deluded souls who actually prefers Robert Bly to William Blake. "God is inside us, all's right with the world" just doesn't have the same ring to it.

Besides, I can't help but notice that the 12 Steps mention a "Higher Power," not an "Inner" one – an understanding of God that's done millions of folks a world of practical good.

I've got lots of people on side, come to think of it, from Simone Weil (with her "gravity and grace") to *The X-Files* ("The Truth Is Out There").

Fashionable or not, I plan to carry on my merry transcendental way. Theologians and psychologists will no doubt have a marvelous time analyzing my preference and dismissing my childish Tridentine paternalism.

But I wonder: when did they last enjoy a guilt-free feast of Chocolate-Chocolate-Chip?

This hereby certifies that...

We read in *The Imitation of Christ* :

Give up this passionate desire for knowledge,
because it distracts you and leads you astray.
Learned people like to be admired and acquire names
for wisdom
yet there are many things which it does little or no good
for a soul to know...
What is the point of a great argument about abstruse
and difficult matters,
when no one will be charged at the Judgement with
being ignorant of them?

I don't know what "abstruse" means either, but the rest sounds good to me, due I suppose to my decidedly unfashionable disdain for theology degrees.

Dave Barry claims that those impressive framed parchments in your doctor's office actually read:

```
THIS   HEREBY   CERTIFIES   THAT

       JOHN    Q.    PUBLIC

HAS  A BIG  PIECE  OF  PAPER

        ON  HIS  WALL
```

That's pretty much how I feel about doctors of any description, medical or academic. I rarely regret my decision to give university a miss. Nevertheless, I do feel a tad gauche in Catholic circles, convinced that people are snickering when I stutter over "Schillebeeckx," or can't remember how we're supposed to pronounce "Nicaragua" this week.

Does that sound familiar? Well, feel stupid no more. After reading the following, you'll know everything theology students learn, in 0.00004% of the time!

The secret?

Vocabulary.

Gone are the days when nuns based illustrious 50-year

careers on two simple sentences: "I trust you've brought a piece of gum for everyone," and "Perhaps you'd like to share your little joke with the rest of us."

Today, they (and you) must memorize the following words in order to be taken even halfway seriously:

- journey
- Christ-event
- paradigm
- broken
- liturgical
- prophetic
- liberation
- discernment
- dialogue
- witness
- formation
- lay

Now, if you can a) squeeze three or more of these words into single sentences, b) do so without laughing, and c) really not laugh, you can pass yourself off as a Real Smart Person. Ditto the straightfaced ease with which you use nouns as verbs, or use nouns in a truly weird way. ("Discern that beautiful sunset!" or "Paradigm the salt, Marjorie.")

But be warned: "lay" has been a tricky English word since Chaucer was a cowboy. *Do Not* inform your mother that you're "going into lay ministry" if there's a family history of strokes. Stick with easier phrases like, "Liberation is the paradigm journey of the Christ-event."

Here's some more handy vocab:

- Apocrypha: Latin for "the good parts."
- Double Effect: what happens when you drink too much.
- Occasions of Sin: only doing it once in a while.
- Vulgate: just sounds like a bad word.
- Titular: a bad word.
- Altar Girl: see above.

Next, spend two weeks in a Southern Hemisphere country, then write five books about your trip.

If you can't afford that, just wear bright, loom-woven clothes from Bridgehead and mutter, "Phew, jet lag!" a lot.

Mutter "Phew, jet lag!" in Spanish and you'll probably be made a Department Head.

Either way, choose a hip, fashionable country to visit (or not). Imagine being halfway through your third autobiography just to hear some fellow working-group member sniff, "India!? How Seventies!" Pick a nation in the midst of a war, in the semi-midst of something vaguely war-ish, or at the very least, one in which the odd fistfight's been known to break out. A culture with cute customs is a must. ("They make the most charming Nativity scenes out of corncobs!")

Armed with this primer in Conversational God-Speak, you can now mingle with perfect perspiration-free poise at any conclave of Professional Catholics.

Meanwhile, here's to all you "real" students out there. I'll be thinking of you as I liberate your reading list out of the library, journey home, formation my feet on the coffee table, and witness *The Beverly Hillbillies.*

Prayer in the days of
plague

Talking to a wall

"WE NEED ALL THE PRAYERS WE CAN GET"

I can't believe I'm reading this in *NOW*, Toronto's hip, far-left weekly famous for its Phone Sex ads – which have fruitfully multiplied along with AIDS: "With more seats in the bar and an interactive jukebox SPEAKEASY lets you mingle from the comfort of your home! ONLY $2.49 a minute!"

Curious callers talking to – each other? Themselves? A wall? Of groans and giggles, or silence?

Those ads shock some, but I'm always more annoyed when *NOW* spells "God" – when they mention God at all – with a lower-case "g."

So this ad shocks me, this half-page *muezzin* call:

WE NEED ALL THE PRAYERS WE CAN GET

IN RECOGNITION OF

World AIDS Day

on December 1,

the Art Gallery of Ontario will open

PAPER PRAYERS

inspired by the Japanese tradition of
offering printed strips of paper as prayers to
sustain good health and cure the sick.

We are asking everyone to submit 4 × 12 inch
works on paper which will be displayed floor to ceiling
over several gallery walls.

I ring the AGO and talk my way into their Paper Prayers press preview.

Writers are glorified eavesdroppers, and that ad (like a cryptic phone call to a Cold War spy) clicks my brain cells into *Mission Impossible* mode.

The Kingdom's keyhole, unobstructed:
What do we say when we pray?

✣ ✣ ✣

"How do you pray?" Bill asks.

For months, Bill and I have passed our pasts on to each other. Histories: familial, vocational, sexual.

But that's his most intimate question yet.

Remembering his Masters in Medieval History strangles my synapses and throat. Afraid of mispronouncing *lectio divina*, I mumble:

"I read stuff, I guess. In the morning."

My prayers, like breakfasts, are soon forgotten – do their daily work, insensible, inside my head and heart: mind-miners, a sweatshop of psalms.

To speak of such things seems unsound – spying on best-left-alone soufflés.

I explain at least that much to Bill. He bakes his own butter tarts; he understands.

Bill reads stuff, too – pulls a tiny *Desert Fathers* from his pocket.

"It's like *How to Deal with Difficult People*," I offer, "but with sand."

Bill proposes a virtual monastery in cyberspace. An on-line order, without walls (or, some might add, contagion). Worldwide would-be Benedictines connected (by computers, not corridors) to others called to recollection, but not to relocation.

After all, the Fathers lived beneath the stars in scattered cells, not beneath the roofs of grand (now quite deserted) cloisters.

"Gives new meaning to 'all things in common,'" I muse, "and compatibility."

But how will we pray with computers?

And will computer viruses be the new heresies?

The media hum viruses as if they're catchy tunes. Turns out, for example, they're the real cause of ulcers. Meanwhile, one last little smallpox colony (awaiting execution at the Center for Disease Control) patiently passes, Shaker-like, its own private eschaton.

There are "news viruses" too – so pundits have dubbed those trivial tales (of figure skaters, football players, Ginsu-wielding wives) that hyperbolize into insatiable mythical beasts, devouring a million times their weight in sound bites to survive. Meanwhile, the documentary narrator says,

"Viruses are pure purpose."

I nod as a talking-head doctor explains that, cured or curbed, one disease just understudies others. A plague by any other name...

I rarely agree with scientists, or with well-meaning souls who say I should thank modern medicine for keeping me alive, if not quite well.

Those people don't have diseases. I do. Chronic, intractable. Like talking to a wall. A wall called "me."

And I am not at all important. I write poetry and get depressed. Who am I to be spared?

What if sickness has a soul, and is holier than I? After all, my overzealous immune system is just acting like any misguided missionary: "Only trying to help..."

"This is the AIDS virus," the narrator says. "It looks like an ornament on a Martian Christmas tree."

✢ ✢ ✢

Simone Weil: "The quantity of evil in the world is precisely equal to the necessary amount of punishment. But it strikes at random."

Much talk these days of "random acts of kindness." And of violence.

Anniversaries, always, like annual colds: Lennon. Salvador. Montreal.

This week, after Jeffrey Dahlmer's murder, Jerry Rubin dies. There's a joke in there somewhere. "Why did the hippie cross the road...?"

And at week's end, the *Sun* imitates the *Enquirer:*

Bouchard Loses Leg to Flesh-Eating Disease

No jokes then, just rumors, spreading like kindergarten coughs: "He lost an arm, too! That's what killed Jim Henson, you know..."

"Sometimes it seems as if the whole world is fueled by gossip," writes Kathleen Norris in *Dakota: A Spiritual Geography*.

If you look up "gossip" in the Oxford English Dictionary, you find that it is derived from the words for God and sibling, and originally meant "akin to God."

Eric Partridge's Origins tells you simply to "see God," and there you find that the word's antecedents include gospel, godspell, sippe (or consanguinity) and "sabha, a village community – notoriously inter-related."

Is Norris onto something with her "holy use of gossip"? A sort of verbal vaccination, homeopathic: (dis)like curing (dis)like? A new strain of intercessory prayer, a benign, benevolent virus?

Dakota is a surprise bestseller. *Newsweek* reports that Norris has "received 3,000 letters from people wanting to share their spiritual lives."

Have we all caught the cosmic cooties?

✣ ✣ ✣

If our prayers all go to the AGO, does that make the AGO heaven?

Can't be: there are EXIT signs. Besides, I'm the first one here.

The Paper Prayers press preview, in the Sculpture Gallery – the AGO's airy atrium afterthought. Cloudlike marble floors, and real clouds above the high glass greenhouse roof.

"I came to a wedding here once," someone says.

Then the exhibit: walls papered with hundreds of prayers. Mostly pictures: holy cards and photocopied photos. Schoolkids' smiling suns.

Mute blues. Reds holding their breath. Pure purpose, wordless desire.

(My friends who pray – that's half of them – would like this silence. Prayer's our not-so-dirty secret; *Dakota* or not, we're still spiritual outlaws in Secular Gulch. Don't want to be mocked, or locked up.)

(We say, "I'll be thinking of you." And mean, "I'll be praying for you." But the latter always sounds less like a blessing than a curse – a smug, contagious, born-again sneeze.)

My writer's eyes need words and had been expecting more here at this exhibit, an explosion in a fortune-cookie factory. Finally I spy some on this not-so-Wailing Wall. I feel otherworldly, unworthy, a germ:

**I KNOW YOUR PAIN IS DONE
AND YOU ARE WITH JOHN**

*see me god
kneeling in prayer
in front of my heater*

SILENCE = DEATH

Mission accomplished, as least for today. Here's how we pray.
Here's what we say:

MONEY FOR TREATMENT

goodnight sweet prince

The resurrection of Ed Wood

Do not depend on the hope of results.
...You may have to face the fact that your work
will be apparently worthless and even achieve
no result at all,
if not perhaps results opposite to what you expect...
As for the big results, these are not in your hands or mine,
but they can suddenly happen...

THOMAS MERTON, *LETTER TO JIM FORREST*

Our story begins, as it should, with an angel bearing glad tidings of brotherhood and peace.

And our hero is a 30-year-old nobody, blessed only with a loyal band of misfit friends and a passion for truth. He dies an ignoble pauper's death.

Then, remarkably, our hero's upside-down story spreads until he's known, even loved, the world over.

You just think you know who I'm talking about.

I'm talking about Ed Wood.

Edward D. Wood, Jr. wrote and directed such '50s Grade Z movies as *Jail Bait* and *I Changed My Sex*: cinematic supermarket tabloids.

Nobody took Ed seriously – possibly because he wore angora sweaters.

Yes, Ed was eccentric, virtually talentless, and always too broke to make even nice-looking bad movies. His drive and imagination far exceeded his skill, means, and vocabulary. The UFOs in Wood's *Plan 9 From Outer Space*, for instance, are just hubcaps dangling from (visible) strings.

And yet, *Plan 9* – a cult classic for 40 years – is now a bestselling video. And if he really was "The Worst Director of All Time," why did he merit *Ed Wood*, an affectionate film biography directed by Tim Burton?

Simply put, Ed loves every second of his stupid sordid life. He gleans pathetic positive nuggets from vicious reviews. ("Look! He liked our costumes!") And when a producer calls Ed's movie the worst he's ever seen, Ed chirps, "And my next one will be even better!"

Ed's as buoyant and resilient as a life preserver. And for one of his friends, he proves to be just that.

Martin Landau won a much-deserved Oscar for his portrayal in *Ed Wood* of horror movie legend Bela Lugosi.

The Lugosi we, and Ed, meet resides in that accursed celebrity limbo in which one is simultaneously world-famous and forgotten; he's on welfare, reduced to watching his old Dracula movies on TV. Alone.

But in Ed's adoring eyes, the withered man is still the Count, the great Lugosi. Ed convinces Bela to star in his next picture.

What an ecstatic Ed doesn't realize is that his new leading man is a morphine addict.

Ed steers Lugosi into rehab, and a grateful Lugosi gives his all for Ed's cheap camera – "wrestling" a broken plastic octopus Ed's "borrowed" from a studio warehouse, Lugosi gamely convinces us that the inert rubber blob is attacking him!

"How do you do it, Ed?" asks Wood's fey friend Bunny. He and Ed are clad in white robes and bobbing in a swimming pool. Seems Ed's convinced some well-heeled Baptists to finance *Plan 9*. They've agreed, on one condition...

"How do you get all your friends baptized," Bunny continues, "just so you can make a horror movie?"

Ed doesn't reply, but we know the answer: faith, hope, and love. Even sultry Vampira turns from enemy to penitent to friend. She rudely brushes Ed off – until she's fired from her TV hostess job. Ed hires her instantly.

"If I judged my friends, I wouldn't have any," he shrugs.

Blessed with the oblivious optimism of the saints, and cursed with their chronic bad luck, a penniless Wood drank himself to death in 1978. His movies survived: minor miracles of bad taste and good intentions, of cardboard sets and crossed fingers, with dialogue once compared to "a ransom note pasted together from words randomly cut out of a Korean electronics manual."

In 1980, two critics dubbed Ed Wood "The Worst Director of All Time." Illustrating Wilde's Law that there's no such thing as bad publicity, that catchy appellation has garnered Ed tremendous posthumous renown.

And in 1994, the ultimate paradox: *Ed Wood*'s budget was one hundred times larger than those of Ed's own films combined. Talk about yer loaves and fishes.

Always the showman, Ed Wood himself might've titled this movie *Jesus of Montreal Meets Sunset Blvd.*

Whatever you call it, judge not, and see how they love one another.

The real hope is not in something we think we can do, but in God who is making something good of it in some way we cannot see.
If we can do His will, we will be helping in this process. But we will not necessarily know all about it beforehand.
THOMAS MERTON, *LETTER TO JIM FORREST*

Plan nice from outer space

There was a clear expectation of saintliness in the air
that afternoon, and toward the end, [Zen master]
Sensei, exasperated by it and wanting to smoke,
lit a cigarette.
Shock, shock. He said, "Must not be narrow."
True spirituality is not in social conventions.

NAN SHIN, *DIARY OF A ZEN NUN*

A saint is someone who loves everyone, not someone whom
everyone loves.

Nevertheless, some people believe that "being holy" is syn-
onymous with "being nice."

"Being nice" may indeed be the culturally approved, bland-leading-the-bland way for quiet, queuing Canadians to behave, especially Canadian women.

But just how are "being nice" and "being Christian" (that is, "countercultural") actually related?

It is not unusual, in the lives of the saints,
to find that saints did not always agree with saints.
Peter did not always agree with Paul, nor Philip Neri
with Charles Borromeo.
And sometimes very holy men have been very exasperating people
and tiresome to live with.

Ah, to have such problems! To live in the days before "conflict resolution."

In the years since Thomas Merton wrote those lines, Catholic culture has lost most of its earthy sensuality, as well as its equally famous flip side: a stringent, sometimes macabre, asceticism.

Art's been reduced to Craft and Creativity; Sanctity to Sabbaticals, Seminars, and Self-Improvement – spawning more Charlie Browns than Charles Borromeos.

Just who is responsible for those "wholesome" whole-wheat Hosts? (King of Kings! Lord of Lords! Good Source of Dietary Fiber!) The same humorless hippie social worker, no doubt, who labeled the lustiest, most confusing time of life "youth" (that smug, anemic excuse for a noun). Ladies and gentlemen: the '70s are over! You aren't going to attract "youth" to the church with your uptight, boring, safe idea of "youth."

Meanwhile, this era's contribution to Catholic philosophy? The Consistent Life Ethic. Only someone who's spent more time in a library than out-of-doors could possibly think that any "life" worth living could possibly be "consistent," let alone want it to be.

I know your deeds; I know you are neither
cold nor hot.
How I wish you were one or the other – hot or cold!
But because you are lukewarm,
neither hot nor cold,
I will spew you out of my mouth!
REVELATION 3:15–16

My Jesus isn't "meek and mild." His coming was proclaimed by a guy who ate bugs, and Jesus himself ran away from home and talked back to his mother.

He turned water into wine – not the other way around.

And he told us to pray for our enemies; he didn't say don't have any.

In other words,
John appeared neither eating nor drinking,
and people say, "He is mad!"
The Son of Man appeared eating and drinking,
and they say, "This one is a glutton and a drunkard,
a lover of tax collectors and those outside the law."
Yet time will prove where wisdom lies.

MATTHEW 11:18–19

Some nice people were shocked to learn that Maya Angelou – the majestic, prayerful, prophetic poet who performed at President Clinton's Inaugural – had, in her youth, run a brothel.

Being a poet myself, I was not.

Passion and pain, not politeness or perfectionism, are the purest crucibles for poetry and prayer.

Sadhu Sundar Singh: "The children of God are very dear but very queer – very nice but very narrow."

A Make Room For Misfits Manifesto is an obvious oxymoron. This little ditty's just a plea for diversity and discernment. The saint and the sinner swap cheat notes, that's all. Remember that stuff about whited sepulchers? About judging not?

Perhaps Simone Weil – that unkempt, chain-smoking nutbar – had the best take on the mere appearance of sanctity: that there's nothing inherently holy about waiting and fasting – any desperate gambler does as much.

The strange fruits of
Schindler's List

If you meet the Buddha on the road, kill him.

ZEN PROVERB

Had I met Oskar Schindler on the road, I might have killed him.

Oskar Schindler was exactly the sort of man I once despised (and sometimes still do): "yuppie scum," a capitalist "suit," a rich old white guy. A profiteer, a drinker, a smoker, a womanizer, a bottom-liner.

In short, a favorite target for my anarcho-peacenik comrades and me.

And if Hitler rose from the dead and took over the world? (Some might say he already has, but that's another story...)

Well, my radical comrades and I would call an emergency

meeting, draft a new mission statement, and brew another batch of Bridgehead coffee in our little basement office.

Meanwhile, over on Bay Street, some latter-day Schindler might use his worldly savvy, questionable connections, and considerable stash of ill-gotten cash to quietly save people's lives.

Behold, I send you out as sheep in the midst of wolves.
Therefore be wise as serpents and harmless as
doves...
Now brother will deliver up brother to death, and a
father his child;
and children will rise up against parents and cause
them to be put to death.
And you will be hated by all for My name's sake.
But he who endures to the end will be saved.
MATTHEW 10:16, 21, 22

I used to read that and think that Jesus was talking about me.

And I once smiled knowingly when recalling that famous exchange in the movie *Annie Hall*:

Diane Keaton's just watched *The Sorrow and the Pity*, a film about the French resistance in the Second World War. She wonders aloud how she'd hold up under torture.

Woody Allen replies that the Nazis would just take away her credit cards and she'd tell them everything.

Because I didn't have charge cards, owned no real property because it was "theft," and was purposely, proudly poor – hell, I would've been a *leader* of the French Resistance, thank you very much...

After watching *Schindler's List* I wondered how I'd hold up under torture. Which side would I really be on?

Scattered amongst us all are hometown prophets, rejected cornerstones. Tax collectors. Prostitutes. There is nothing nice about them. They don't attend meditation workshops and peace conferences. They are too busy living, or trying to live, to worry and wonder if they're doing it "right."

Some die penniless (as Schindler did) or slip on the banana peels of addiction, passion, even greed. Shaggy, sloe-eyed rock stars. Temperamental painters. Cranky clowns. They aren't always sober or celibate, pacifist or poor.

God hands the Ten Commandments to a murderer named Moses, and the Twelve Steps to a bankrupt stockbroker. A randy king called David writes the Psalms. St. Augustine prays *make me pure, but not yet.*

My TV is on while I write this.

The Very Reverend Somebody-Or-Other is being interviewed. He's at Westminster Abbey, where another Oscar (Wilde that is) is finally being granted a place in Poet's Corner.

"We do not judge individuals by their morality or lack thereof," intones the Very Reverend, the royal red carpet of his High Church vowels rolled out for this special occasion, "but by their contribution to literature."

After the news, a documentary about Billie Holiday. Nothing nice about Lady Day, either. Addicted and promiscuous, she wore a big gaudy gardenia behind her ear and sang, "Ain't nobody's business if I do…"

She also sang *Strange Fruit*, a song about lynching. Also not nice. A song that probably saved more lives than many a hand-wringing meeting of guilty white liberals.

Radicals claim to witness a kingdom come, a world turned upside down. I once blabbed on about how the root of the word "radical" is, well, "root." Today I see that there's a nasty implication in there somewhere, to the effect that roots are somehow more important than, say, flowers.

Oskar Schindler's flashy boutonniere.

Oscar Wilde's limp, outrageous lily.

Billie Holiday's gardenia.

Loud lusty flowers that bloom too big and bright and die too soon.

Imagine a garden of nothing but roots. If that's "the world turned upside down," you can have it.

The Father, Son and Dolly Parton

Bonfire of the vanities

God runs a beauty parlor.

NORMAN VINCENT PEALE

When I was very little, I played with my mother's Bible.

I also fashioned heavy, easy-to-trip-over "habits" from blankets and sheets, a tea-towel "veil" bobbypinned to my four-year-old head, and played nun.

No loaf of Wonder Bread was safe from my pinching fingers, as I squished slice after slice into bite-sized "hosts."

And I much preferred "holy" statues to Barbies. True, you couldn't change Joseph's hair or Mary's outfit, but that didn't stop me from concocting elaborate adventures starring my nativity scene "dolls."

But that Bible: like my mother's evening bag, it was black and shiny, with a bright gold zipper.

Instead of Kleenex, however, the book contained pages. On a special glossy one marked DEATHS, someone's unmistakably Scottish – and touchingly misspelled – scrawl: *Grandfarther Shaidle.*

And, instead of lipstick, it contained words, TRANSLATED OUT OF THE ORIGINAL TONGUES: SELF-PRONOUNCING EDITION.

And, instead of powder puffs, pictures: Noah's ark bulging like a wooden bicep, complete with rainbow tattoo; a scowling, red-robed, white-bearded Moses (I think the unthinkable: an angry Santa) throwing what looks like a granite drive-in menu from *The Flintstones* at some guy's turbaned head; Jesus, just as angry, DRIVING OUT THE SOMEBIGWORD, a broken cage of doves at his feet and the doves flying out. I'd seen caged doves at a birthday party. Was Jesus a magician, too?

More birthdays and birds. The last picture: PENTECOST. Whatever that was. Another dove, and birthday-candle-people, flames on their heads, yet strangely unafraid.

Sitting in a row like that (their faces surprised, delighted – all trying to speak at once) the picture-people remind me of the ladies I see every Friday when my mother takes me with her to the beauty parlor:
the picture-people sitting under tongues-of-fire hair dryers, shouting to be heard;

those little flames, too, like the amber pilot lights on coffee urns
and curling irons;

like, in winter, the scary, molten-steel space heater they plug in
near the cash register (a fire so frightening it needs its own cage;
like a burning bush) – boots huddle around it, drying out;

like the blazing brush of red dye the hairdresser daubs on my
mother's scalp with one crimson-nailed hand; in the other, a
fluttering, glowing cigarette she uses like a punctuation mark:
"so I says to him I says... "

Except, of course, that most of the people in the PENTE-
COST picture aren't ladies.

Which, luckily, I don't even notice until years later.

Dolly Parton: "If I hadn't been a star I would've been a beauti-
cian or a missionary."

Now there are varieties of gifts, but the same Spirit.

A man I saw years ago on Vision/TV, a Zoroastrian and professional hairdresser, had developed a unique spare-time ministry: giving free make-overs to battered women.

He styled their long-neglected hair, massaged their scalps,
covered up bruises. As the only man allowed, even welcomed,
in the shelters he visited, this hairdresser had an awesome re-
sponsibility: to earn the women's trust (to let him, after all, hold

scissors so close to their faces); to show them that a man's hands could heal as well as hurt.

"Show" because words, empty twisted words, had let these women down before; callous words had slapped them. That he knew he was a nice guy wasn't enough, and saying so meant even less. So this modest man spoke with his brush and comb.

He shrugged off the praise he received for his volunteer work.

"My religion asks me to use my talents to help others," he said quietly. "And I am a hairdresser."

Send forth your Spirit, O Lord
And renew the face of the earth.

It's 29 all over again

My hamster died on my birthday.

"I see a cage without an owner. It is an ex-hamster. It has ceased to be!" I whimpered, having called Suzanne to whine about this depressing turn of events. She tried to cheer me up by telling me about a friend of hers who woke up Christmas morning to find the lifeless body of her brand-new, white Persian kitten lying under the living room tree.

It says a lot about me that I found that anecdote utterly hilarious, but when I finally stopped laughing I was once again dancing cheek to cheek with toe-crushing reality: "turning 29" was bad enough; "dead rodent disposal" was something else again, and, I hoped, not a portent of things to come.

My 29th birthday was a major milestone; it was, after all, the only one I'd be celebrating for the next ten years. If you'd told me a decade ago that I'd one day be indulging in that dubious female tradition of "birthday manipulation," I'd have hit you with my copy of *The Second Sex* (the one with "How true!" scrawled up the margins in red ink). For I Was A Teenage Feminist, with more hair on my legs than on top of my head, and a very low vanity threshold.

But *sic transit gloria steinem...*

Besides, men do it too. The *TV Guide*'s "Specials" section reveals that Bob Hope has about 17 birthdays a year. Then there's Pete Townsend, who once said, "I hope I die before I get old." Given some of his post-Who solo work, it's a shame he didn't get his wish.

If Pete Townsend can be a professional adolescent, why can't I? At least long enough to deliver my speech to that upcoming conference of teenagers with lupus. Why should they listen to a woman who, until last Tuesday, thought Pearl Jam was a rap group? That I'm the same age as the actors who play high school students on *Beverly Hills 90210* only exacerbates my sense of creeping old-fogey-ism.

My birthday wasn't exactly a "call-out-the-National-Guard" level disaster. My mother and grandmother traveled from Hamilton to visit me, toting enough food, laundry detergent, and toilet paper to stock an aircraft carrier. We passed the time with some scintillating Shaidle Family Banter:

Mom: Kathy's guppy died.

Me: Hamster.

Grandma: What?

Mom: I said–

Grandma: I heard you. The gerbil.

Me: Hamster.

Mom: What?

Following that production of *The Importance of Being Earnest*, we went out for dinner and had a real nice time. (Thanks, Mom.)

The next evening, more dinner was had at Suzanne's. The conversation was slightly higher up on the food chain, even if, like all good friends, Suzanne and I just have the very same conversation over and over again: "For which celebrity would you agree to work as his/her Personal Assistant/Groveling Scum Toadie for absolutely free?" ("Cher.") etc., etc.

"Cher" was, as usual, the answer to every question. Perhaps getting old isn't so bad, I mused, since Cher, not to mention Joan Collins, Dolly Parton and dozens of others have made it fashionable to be over 30 and female. Unfortunately, (as triumphs of strategic shoulder-padding over chronology) Cher, Joan Collins, and Dolly Parton also share a remarkable resemblance to men in drag – a rather tired observation, the implications of which are perhaps best left unexamined.

While still in their 20s, T. S. Eliot had written *Prufrock*; the *Beyond the Fringe* troupe was the toast of Broadway; and Thérèse of Lisieux had pulled off a beautiful, tubercular death in the grand tradition of French popular piety. I have little to show for my first three decades other than a complete collection of *Blackadder* episodes and a leopardskin-print umbrella.

What's more – at least according to Abbie Hoffman – next year I won't even be able to trust myself. Too bad Abbie was the one who got Pete Townsend's famous wish. Maybe he's up there taking care of my hamster.

What's so funny 'bout peace, love, and total silence?

Silent Retreat notes, Advent 1995:

Being spiritual was easier before I got a job.

The job I just started – the intense, demanding job I'm so proud, scared, and lucky to have, the job that brought me to this convent, for an already much-needed weekend rest – has made me the last to arrive, at 6 p.m.

The others are gingerly, silently, finishing their dinner as I begin. A nun sweeps toward me. I naturally assume that I am already In Big Trouble.

"Sorry! Late!" I blurt, my mouth crumbly with homemade bread.

"You aren't late, dear, you're just eating your dinner," she replies sweetly.

You learn to talk like that at Nun School. Even Anglican Nun School, I guess.

A bell signals the end of dinner. Chairs scrape across the floor. Only my plate isn't empty. Assuming I'd break one of St. Benedict's rules by wasting food, I furtively shove a forlorn slice of Swiss cheese into my pocket and follow the others out the door – here just an hour before me and already suave veterans.

We shuffle into a quaint beige sitting room, the incongruous focal point of which is a big-screen TV that looks jarringly like the mute, judgmental monolith in *2001*.

Before The Great Silence begins its 30-hour reign, we watch a documentary about meditation.

The affable clergyman who's leading our retreat seems a tiny bit overwhelmed by the enormous TV and its equally friendly sidekick, the VCR.

It's my turn to be taken aback when said clergyman introduces us to his wife.

Robin Williams calls The Church of England "Catholic Lite – all the pomp without the guilt."

Yet there's nothing "lite" about it. As far as "light" is concerned, however, this exists abundantly.

During Morning Prayer, I sneak not-so-discreet glances at the poised and perfectly postured pray-ers, and simply cannot imagine them doing anything secretive, superstitious..."Mediterranean." Saints Rose of Lima or Maria Goretti wouldn't last long around here. Come to think of it, they didn't last long in the first place.

Despite this crisp, o-so-sane liturgy (or perhaps because of it) I'm in no danger of converting: I can't sing a note, and certainly can't afford the apparently prerequisite elocution lessons.

That said, I'm pleased to discover, as the morning goes on, that my cheeky, pre-retreat suspicions were correct: 30 years of Lindsay Anderson films and Monty Python skits really *did* prepare me to fake my way through an Anglican service without irreparably humiliating myself.

Amusing what startles one: I live in a Toronto neighborhood in which men wearing women's clothing (and looking better in them than I do) are a fairly common sight.

So I'm sitting in the chapel, eyes closed, thinking about the latest controversies about women's ordination and infallibility, and I open my eyes, and notice a woman sitting across from me, with her eyes closed.

And she's wearing a clerical collar.

And my gut reaction is: ugh.

Aesthetic response or philosophical one? Evidence of self-loathing or just fear of the unknown?

Reassuringly, a convent is a convent, on whatever shore of the Tiber: doilies everywhere; spindly-legged mahogany tables; pea-soup shag carpeting – the mismatched furniture of dubious pedigree coming together anyhow, like those freakish families on TV who adopt 35 kids from all over.

And what would a convent be without plants: radiant African violets that only church ladies can grow, and of course, That Philodendron. You know the one I mean: 100 years old, with leaves like yellow dinosaur teeth; no doubt a direct descendant of one Elijah grew on Mount Carmel.

Day Two: interestingly, the silence seems to be affecting our inner ears. I've never careened into so many people – bumps and jostles and muffled verboten "sorry"s are an embarrassing hallway commonplace. I came here to forget myself, but am becoming more self-conscious rather than less so.

That night I hear a couple of short sharp animal roars, peek out my door to investigate, and spot the source: another bathrobed retreatant shuffles back to her room, two Kleenex in hand, freshly (and o-so-loudly) plucked from the pink box on the table across the way.

Sunday morning, and a second helping of the best oatmeal I've ever eaten. And yet...normally, right about now, I'd be eating Philip's oatmeal, on a little tray, breakfast in bed. His oatmeal isn't as good as this oatmeal, but then we don't date for culinary reasons.

Only a few hours to go, and I've had a wonderful time here, but...

While stealth is patently unnecessary, I still feel obliged to "sneak" into the convent's narrow indoor telephone booth to call in for a weekend's worth of messages.

A friend wonders where I've been. A magazine editor wants two of my poems.

The third caller doesn't say hello, or even leave his name. He doesn't have to. At first all I hear are dry, discordant whistles, but seconds later they settle into a recognizable tune:

The Sound of Silence.

Seems Philip didn't want to somehow break my vow of silence by speaking into my answering machine.

I decide not to stay for dinner that night, hurriedly pack, express my thanks to the sisters, and stagger through the unshoveled suburban snow to the subway, and home.

Familiar sounds, like a bus splashing slush, clang in my empty ears. My mind feels just as empty, searches for, and finally finds, the expression I want: "the bends."

Like a diver rising to the surface, I ache to return to the earth.

God rides a Yamaha

"I suppose they try and make you believe an awful lot of nonsense?"

"Is it nonsense? I wish it were. It sometimes sounds terribly sensible to me."

"But my dear Sebastian, you can't seriously believe it all?"

"Can't I?"

"I mean about Christmas and the star and the three kings and the ox and the ass."

"Oh yes, I believe that. It's a lovely idea."

"But you can't believe things because they're a lovely idea."

"But I do. That's how I believe."

EVELYN WAUGH, *BRIDESHEAD REVISITED*

✤ ✤ ✤

Philip rides a motorcycle.

That's not the first thing his sister told me about him.

"He's very intelligent and cute and he works in computers and writes songs and plays hockey – but you know, once I called him 'a Renaissance man' and he didn't know what that meant."

That whimsical coda piqued my interest, but the bike cinched it. Ahhh, imagine buzzing my (recently) ex-boyfriend's place, on the back of a growling Harley...

Okay, so Philip's bike turned out to be a Yamaha – but it *is* purple, which covereth a multitude of sins.

For someone who can't drive a car, or even ride a bicycle, I'm pretty snotty, I know. What's more remarkable: that someone as devoutly sedentary as Yours Truly has gone "hog wild."

(Or not: after all, what's motorcycling anyhow but sitting down – really, really fast?)

Last summer, we drove all over. Through the streets of Toronto – dueling with truckers, cyclists, rollerbladers, even tourist-toting rickshaws; sliding into coveted, subatomic parking spaces right in front of theaters and cafes. Along major highways and sinewy country roads – one autumn night, driving into a harvest moon that was poised like a Ferris wheel on a farmer's field.

I wear a red helmet, a leather jacket, gloves and boots, and become the tough broad I just pretend, unconvincingly, to be the rest of the time.

In reality, we've survived only one marginally dangerous encounter: a yobbo took mysterious exception to Philip's aging collegiate leather jacket.

"Look guys," he yelled to his gang as Philip and I climbed on the bike, "pretty boy went to Waterloo!"

Philip swiveled his helmeted head around to me and murmured, "Let's get out of here before he sees the word MATH on my arm."

Now it's February, and I'm waiting impatiently for the roads to thaw, but when I think about riding with Philip again, sometimes I get a little sad.

Not because dating someone who's smarter and better looking than I am is a decidedly exciting yet humiliating experience. (He yelled "Rutherford's atom?!" when my aunt drew a circle on the Pictionary board.)

Indeed, certain alert Catholic readers no doubt read my initial descriptive paragraphs and are preparing to mail Philip some Jesuit recruitment brochures.

Unfortunately for vocation directors everywhere, Philip doesn't believe in celibacy.

And unfortunately for me, he doesn't believe in God.

Philip and I have many other differences, mostly temperamental: mind-sets that are anecdotal versus analytical, experiential versus experimental.

But The God Thing is a different, deeper matter. To date, we've signed a shaky truce: I don't "happen" to leave *Surprised by Joy* in the bathroom, and Philip, well, he simply doesn't say anything much.

What he does say displays a sensitivity which is far more common among atheists than believers. "God's looking after you," he told me, when I couldn't find a job, or had to visit the doctor (again).

And I cheer up, but it feels like he's calling me long distance, from Australia or someplace, reassuring his depressed Canadian girlfriend on the other end of the line that the sun will rise any second now – even though it's midnight at his end.

We don't live on separate planets so much as in different time zones. And that can't go on forever.

But hey, we biker chicks live in the "now," man, so I'll cross that bridge when I come to it. On a Yamaha or not.

KATHY SHAIDLE has been publishing poetry, fiction, essays and reviews since 1984. Her work has appeared in *Seventeen*, *The London Free Press*, *America*, and in a variety of anthologies. Her columns for *Catholic New Times* won four Canadian Church Press awards, including Best National Columnist. Her poetry collection *Lobotomy Magnificat* was published by Oberon in 1997. She was diagnosed with systemic lupus erythematosus (SLE) in 1991.